A Practical Business Guide for

Church Planning & Community Outreach

Dawnette Blackwood-Rhoomes

A Practical Business Guide for
Church Planning & Community Outreach
by Dawnette Blackwood-Rhoomes

Copyright © 2024 Dawnette Blackwood-Rhoomes

All rights reserved. No part of this book may be used or reproduced by any means, graphic, electronic, or mechanical, including photocopying, recording, taping or by any information storage retrieval system without the written permission of the publisher except in the case of brief quotations embodied in critical articles and reviews.

Scriptures quoted are taken from the New International Version (NIV) of the Holy Bible.

A DBRPub Publication
dbrdesigns1@gmail.com

Printed in the United States of America by Amazon
ISBN: 9798321748824

All rights reserved.
Cover Design Layout by YaniDwi | Canva.com.
Graphics by Canva.com

DBRPub

Acknowledgement

In recognition of the need within our church body for more community outreach programs, I would like to take this opportunity to express my gratitude to leaders and officers of churches who work tirelessly to support community engagement.

Contents

Introduction		7
Chapter 1	The Mission & Vision Statements	10
Chapter 2	The Planning Committee	18
Chapter 3	Garnering the Church's Feedback	22
Chapter 4	Goals	27
Chapter 5	Creating a Goal-Oriented Church Culture	32
Chapter 6	Assessing the Church's Position (SWOT)	34
Chapter 7	The Planning Budget	39
Chapter 8	The Marketing of Community Outreach	51
Chapter 9	Marketing Channels for the Church	55
Chapter 10	Scoreboard (Performance Overview)	62
Chapter 11	Practical Community Outreach Exercises	68
Chapter 12	Conclusion	83
References		85

INTRODUCTION

The primary use of this book is to serve as a practical resource and guide for church leadership in their implementation of the concepts and strategies discussed. It includes strategic planning for both the church and community outreach, marketing tools, and the appropriate use of KPIs to evaluate and assess the success of community programs.

Churches today must navigate a dynamic landscape of staying true to their spiritual mission and objectives while employing the strategies and tactfulness of the business world to engage the community, retain membership, and reach new audiences. While this is easier said than done, church leaders must be grounded in service with the determination to drive the church's mission in meeting the needs of the community. This book is educational and informative, teaching church leaders how to make a greater impact by employing an organic and holistic business approach to fulfill core mission and values. The key elements of mission, vision, and goals are complemented in the utilization of the SWOT analysis to optimize the aspirations and desired outcomes of the church's efforts. Further, by employing budgeting, marketing strategies, and success indicators, church leaders can effectively allocate resources, leverage various channels to offer their initiatives to diverse audiences, and measure the success and impact of their plans with meaningful indicators.

Learning Outcomes

Upon completion of reading this guide, pastors, church elders, and officers will be able to:
1. Develop proficiency in constructing and refining short, medium, and long-term strategic goals that align with their mission and vision for church planning and for community outreach efforts.
2. Identify and address factors contributing to growth stagnation within the church community.

3. Assess outcomes and recognize opportunities for advancement and improvement with the use of a SWOT analysis.
4. Demonstrate competency in utilizing strategic analysis and decision-making tools and frameworks to devise effective solutions to community outreach related issues, needs and challenges.
5. Acquire the skills necessary to implement strategies effectively, fostering a culture within the church that is oriented toward achieving established goals and objectives.

While the church is not a business, it can utilize strategic planning and effective management practices to elevate its mission, foster engagement in community outreach initiatives, and create a sustainable goal-oriented church culture.

How to Use This Guidebook
There are 3 options available:
1. This book can be used on its own as a guide to improving the leadership and officers' responsibilities within your faith-based and non-profit organizations.
2. For a deeper learning experience, inclusive of case study and assignments, use this book with *"A Practical Business Guide for Church Planning & Community Outreach - Capacity Building Series Workbook"*, also sold on Amazon.
3. For group development and training, get the entire series which includes complimentary copies of the guidebook, the workbook, videos, and PowerPoint presentations for workshops. More details about workshops and training available at https://dbrpub.com

Dawnette Blackwood-Rhoomes

CHAPTER ONE

THE MISSION & VISION STATEMENTS

The intent of the mission and vision statements is to define the primary purpose of the church, its goals, and to determine its core value-system and beliefs or guiding principles.

Deciding on the mission and value-system of your church is the first and most valid exercise of church planning.

These statements communicate the church's identity and primary purpose of the church to its members and the surrounding communities.

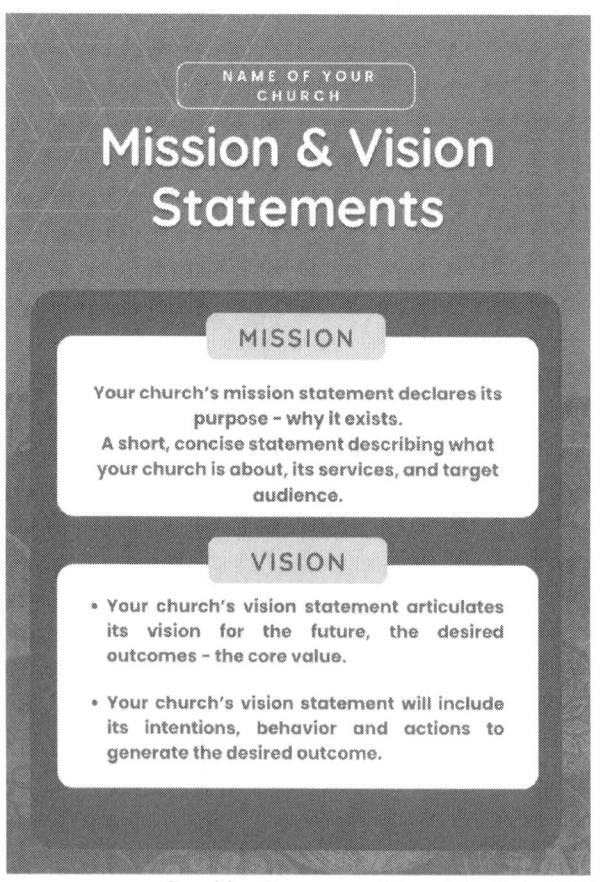

NAME OF YOUR CHURCH

Mission & Vision Statements

MISSION

Your church's mission statement declares its purpose – why it exists.
A short, concise statement describing what your church is about, its services, and target audience.

VISION

- Your church's vision statement articulates its vision for the future, the desired outcomes – the core value.

- Your church's vision statement will include its intentions, behavior and actions to generate the desired outcome.

Graphic: Canva.com (Puput Studio), 2024.

The following is a step-by-step guide on writing the mission and vision statements:

The Mission Statement
1. *Understand the Purpose of the Church* – a pastor who fully understands the purpose of the church to its members and the community will be able to answer the following questions:
   - What do you aim to achieve?
   - What problems are you solving, or what value will the church be providing to its members and the community?
2. *Identify Core Values* – the fundamental principle that guides the church's value-system will remain constant, regardless of both internal and external changes.
3. *Consider the Church's Stakeholders* – your mission and vision statements should take all stakeholders of the church into consideration. Therefore, how will your purpose, goals and objectives affect the church officers, any investors, the members, the surrounding neighborhood, and communities. How will the church contribute to their well-being or address their needs?
4. *Be Concise* – your mission statement should have clarity, and to achieve this, it should be kept short and simple. Therefore, it will be a brief, well-focused and free of jargon declaration of the church's purpose.
5. *Inspire and Motivate* – create a statement that inspires your members, one in which they can relate and align to.
6. *Here are the key elements needed for a mission statement:*
   - Begin with the purpose or what your church aims to achieve.
   - Mention the key stakeholders, such as the church officers, members, and communities.
   - Declare the unique aspects or value your church offers.
7. *Review and Refine* – It is important to get feedback from key stakeholders and revise the statement accordingly. While it's not necessary to interview the entire church body in this regard, a sample population such as the planning committee would be an ideal reflection of the members' interests.

Crafting the Mission Statement

It is a given that when crafting the mission statement for the church, the spiritual aspect should be included.

While there is no strict formula for writing the mission statement, this can be used as a starting point:

Action Verb + Target + Outcome + Qualifier

For example:
To *action verb* + *target* + by *outcome* + with *qualifier*

Action Verbs: These are dynamic words that convey movement, purpose, and action. In the context of a mission statement, action verbs would highlight what the church intends to do, using such verbs as "dedicate", "inspire" educate" or "empower".

Target: The target specifies the group of people the church wishes to be the recipients of their services, such as the church members and the community.

Outcome: The desired result or impact of the church's actions, initiatives, or programs is described in the outcome. The outcome should be specific and measurable. For example, you can use phrases such as "strengthened relationships", "increased enrichment", and "enhanced social culture".

Qualifier: This part of the statement is additional information used to enhance the outcome, using phrases such as "with compassion", "by promoting diversity", and "based on Christian principles". We use qualifiers to stand out as unique and purposeful.

Here's a sample mission statement (with a tagline) for a church:

"Rooted in Faith, Nurturing Community, Serving Humanity

*At [Church Name], we are dedicated **to** fostering a vibrant, loving community centered on the teachings of Christ **by** creating a welcoming spiritual home **with** our inclusive family programs, which enrich the lives of our church officers, members, and the broader community."*

The above-mentioned mission statement is a general one, and yours should be customized based on the specific purpose, goals, and objectives of your church community.

Here are some goals and objectives that can be included in the mission statement:
1. Nurturing Spiritual Growth
2. Building a Supportive Community
3. Empowering Church Officers
4. Serving the Broader Community
5. Fostering Unity and Inclusivity
6. Transformative Worship and Education
7. Striving for Social Justice

While there is not a strict formula for writing a mission statement, there are some common elements and guidelines that can help structure and guide the process. In crafting your mission statement, consider including the following components:

- *Purpose or Mission* – stating the purpose or mission of the church provides clarity for your stakeholders.
- *Values* – core values guide the church's behavior and decision-making, which therefore creates and defines the church's social culture.
- *Customers or Stakeholders* – state who are your stakeholders.
- *Your Offer to Your Stakeholders* – briefly talk about your offer to the members and the community.
- *Differentiation* – you can also consider stating how your church is different in its approach.
- *Inspiration/Motivation* – your statement should inspire and motivate stakeholders.
- *Conciseness* – keeping your statement brief and focused on the main points is good for comprehension.
- *Alignment* – don't forget mission statements must also align with your organization's values, goals, and long-term vision.

The Vision Statement
1. *Identify Core Values* – core values in regard to the Value Statement points to the fundamental beliefs and principles

that govern or guide the church in decision-making and corporate behavior.
2. *Align with Mission* – the core values must align with the purpose of the church. The values should, therefore, help to achieve the vision.
3. *Prioritize Values* – identify the most important values that are non-negotiable. These establish guidelines for stakeholders.
4. *Define Behaviors* – determine how the values can be translated into the day-to-day behaviors of the stakeholders. These values would be embodied in the members' work.
5. *Communicate Internally and Externally* – share the values with members and the community to communicate what the church stands for.
6. *Here are the key elements needed for a vision statement:*
   - List the core values with brief explanations.
   - Relate each value to specific behaviors or actions.
   - Emphasize the importance of these values in achieving the outcome.
7. *Regularly Reinforce* – There should be a purpose to the vision statement to help with reinforcement and to create church culture and decision-making.

Crafting the Vision Statement

As with the mission statement, when crafting the church's vision statement, the spiritual aspect should also be included.

Also, there is no strict formula for writing the vision statement, but you can use this as a starting point:

At [Organization] we value +
[Core Value 1] (Brief Explanation – Give Behavior & Action)
+
[Core Value 2] (Brief Explanation – Give Behavior & Action)
+
[Core Value 3] (Brief Explanation – Give Behavior & Action)

Core Value 1: Normally, the core values of the organization are listed in the vision statement. You can have more than one core value as a representation of the church's beliefs, ideals, and standards. Examples of core values might include integrity, compassion, and dedicated service.

Brief Explanation of Behavior & Action: This component briefly describes a manifesto of the church's intentions, behavior, and actions regarding the core value. As a result, the statement is not only aspirational but also directional (serves as a guide for future decisions and actions).

Here's a sample mission statement (with a tagline) for a church:

"Guided by Faith, United in Love, Serving with Compassion

At [Church Name], we value Christ as our foundation to ground us in love, have unity in spirit to foster a culture of acceptance and service, and a community that embraces and uplifts all."

The above-mentioned vision statement is a general one, and yours should be customized based on the specific beliefs, principles and core-values and culture of your church community.

Here are some principles and core-values that can be included in the vision statement:
1. Faith-Centered Living
2. Unconditional Love
3. Integrity and Accountability
4. Empowering Leadership
5. Inclusive Community
6. Compassionate Service
7. Lifelong Learning
8. Prayerful Guidance

Like the mission statement, there are common elements to consider for crafting your vision statement:

- *Identify Your Cores* – make sure to state the core beliefs and principles to shape culture and behavior.
- *Explanation of Each Value* – briefly give details of each value, thereby creating a common understanding.
- *Alignment with Mission* – the vision statement must align with the mission of the church. This reinforces the church's overall objectives.

- *Behaviors and Actions* – How do you expect each value to translate into behavior? Write clear expectations of stakeholders' attitudes.
- *Priority* – state the values that are more essential and central to your church's outlook first.
- *Connect to Stakeholders* – each value should be relatable to the stakeholders.
- *Consistency* – values should be consistent through the day-to-day activities of the church.
- *Relevance to Industry or Sector* – of course, your values should reflect the expectations of the church and resonate with its members.

Finally, both the mission and value statements should be living documents, which are revisited and revised regularly to maintain the social culture of the church.

In the Bible we see that Jesus had a mission for his ministry, to spread the good news of the God's kingdom to all and to redeem mankind back to the Father. In Luke 4:18-19, Jesus spoke about his intended outcome, which is to bring good news to the poor, freedom to the prisoners, healing to the blind, and liberation to the oppressed; and his visionary outlook for the church in his command to "go and make disciples" (Matthew 28:19a, NIV).

EXERCISE: Create your church's mission and vision statements.

_____
_____
_____
_____
_____
_____
_____
_____
_____
_____
_____
_____
_____
_____
_____
_____
_____
_____
_____
_____
_____

CHAPTER TWO

THE PLANNING COMMITTEE

A church's planning committee consists of a group of nominated and elected members of the church body, who are tasked with the responsibility of overseeing and coordinating the strategic planning process. The primary role of this committee is to assist the pastor in facilitating, developing, implementing, and monitoring the church's strategic plan.

A new pastor usually enters a church with his agenda, already having an idea of the plans he has in mind. However, if he is open to suggestions and ideas, and is willing to understand and connect with his congregation, he establishes a strong foundation for effective leadership and shared ownership and fosters a collaborative and inclusive atmosphere.

To do this, the pastor must institute a planning committee to act as a sample of the church population. He will work closely with this group, whose key role is to ensure the church's objectives are achieved. This includes the following activities and responsibilities:

1. *Strategic Planning* – lead in the development of the strategic plan which embodies defining the mission, vision, goals, and objectives that will guide the church's activities over a decided period of time.
2. *Analysis* – both the pastor and planning committee should conduct a thorough analysis of the stakeholders and the church's positioning.
   - First begin with internal stakeholders, such as the officers and members of the church. This is a process of getting to know everyone, as well as garnering opinions and suggestions to gauge the attitude climate of the congregation via a survey. The following factors should be taken into consideration:
     - *What are the talents and skills that can be utilized to enhance church growth?*

- *What are the current plans and intentions in place?*
- *What improvements can be made to these plans?*
- *Is there youth participation and are their opinions and perspectives taken into consideration?*

- The planning committee can further analyze the external stakeholders, such as its surrounding neighborhoods or communities, to gain perspective on the expectations of the community (also done by a survey).
- To determine the church's positioning to its stakeholders, the planning committee must develop a SWOT Analysis to identify the church's strengths, weaknesses, opportunities, and threats (more on this later).

3. *Goal Setting* – It's important to establish specific, measurable, achievable, relevant, and time-bound (SMART) goals that align with the church's mission and vision.
4. *Resource Allocation* – To achieve the goals and objectives, sufficient resources (time, money, and people) must be allocated. Therefore, the planning committee must take into account the church's budget, the skills and talents of its members to make up a capable body of church officers, and technology.
5. *Communication and Engagement* – It is the responsibility of the committee to effectively communicate the strategic plan to the various departments of the church, and to engage with the officers to foster understanding and commitment.
6. *Monitoring and Evaluation* – Plans must always be monitored, and key performance indicators (KPIs) put in place to track the initiative's progress. The committee is also responsible for reporting if there are adjustments to the initiative or plan, and to collectively make the adjustments.
7. *Risk Management* – The planning committee must also be able to identify the potential risks and challenges which may affect the success of the plan. Risk mitigation plans are important.

8. *Adaptation and Flexibility* – There must be some level of flexibility in all plans. This helps the planning committee to appropriately adjust in response to changes in the congregation's viewpoint, etc.
9. *Creating a Culture through daily actionable* steps – The creation of church culture is paramount to the success of the mission and vision of the church. It determines the attitude and behavior of the stakeholders, and this is achieved by translating strategic goals into daily actionable steps.
10. *Reporting to Leadership and Stakeholders* – Progress reporting and updates to the pastor, board members, and the stakeholders provides transparency and builds trust. It's an important role of the planning committee.

Don't underestimate the value of the planning committee. It serves as a collaborative forum for decision-making, and it ensures that strategic plans are executed appropriately, run smoothly, and monitored effectively for the church's mission and vision to be achieved.

There can be various types of planning committees for varying departments of the church. Of course, this is dependent on the size of the church membership. For instance, small churches do not need more than one planning committee.

- *Worship Planning Committee:* Responsible for coordinating worship services, including youth ministry worship services that may often happen outside the church walls.
- *Event Planning Committee:* Responsible for various social events and programs.
- *Finance Planning Committee:* Oversees the financial budgeting and fundraising efforts for outreach campaigns.
- *Building Planning Committee:* Most churches have a building planning committee to monitor and manage the upkeep of the church building.
- *Community Outreach Committee*: Responsible for developing and implementing various outreach programs and community service initiatives.

- *Education Committee:* Coordinates all the church's educational programs and classes for all age groups.
- *Strategic Planning Committee:* Although most churches don't have a strategic planning committee per se, it is good to note that this committee is responsible for developing long-term goals and strategic plans for the church. One way to ensure that this valuable resource is implemented is to integrate a Strategic Planning Officer on the church committee if there are not enough personnel to create an actual strategic planning committee.
- *Safety and Security Committee:* As with all organizations, there is usually a person or a committee that addresses matters of safety and security of church facilities, its members, and visitors. This includes emergency and safety training.

We can easily compare Jesus' twelve disciples to the church's planning committee and understand the need for leaders to delegate and train. Jesus carefully selected his team of twelve who had diverse skills, perspectives, and backgrounds. He involved them in decision-making and strategic planning. He trained them for leadership and ministry, healing, and serving others (Mark 6:7-13, Luke 10:1-20). No pastor is alone. The work of the ministry is a collaborative one.

CHAPTER THREE

GARNERING THE CHURCH'S FEEDBACK

Feedback is crucial to the development, execution, and implementation of any plan. The stakeholder's opinions, suggestions, and ideas are vital in gauging the attitudes of the very people for which your program or initiative is created.

An effective tool to garner overall feedback from church members is to employ the use of a survey or questionnaire. Here is the necessary information needed for the survey:

- *Demographic Information:* By including demographic data such as age, it is good to know what age group of your members favor or are not in favor of a specific initiative.
- *Perceptions of Current State:* The best way to know if the current programs are effective is actually to ask your members about them. Getting their perspectives via a survey not only saves time but is an effective way to rate the impact of each program. Church leaders can use this method to assess the strengths and weaknesses of the programs with the use of qualitative open-ended questions to garner perspectives on satisfaction.
- *Priorities:* Requesting the church's feedback helps church leaders to understand the priorities of the church from their stakeholder's perspective. In other words, they can prioritize such things as spiritual growth, community outreach, and discipleship.
- *Feedback on Past Initiatives:* Church leaders can garner what elements worked in past initiatives and what didn't. This way, they are able to make more informed decisions on the current initiative.
- *Visions & Goals:* We can use surveys and questionnaires to assess whether church members are on board with the church's vision and goals.
- *Communication & Engagement:* By including open-ended questions, respondents can share their thoughts

freely. This provides an opportunity for the planning committee to better understand members' viewpoints.

By structuring the survey in this way, you can gather comprehensive feedback to make more informed decisions, as well as indicate to members that their opinions are important and relevant.

Importance of Gathering Feedback

Getting feedback from stakeholders in general fosters a culture of inclusivity in which there is a collaborative effort between leaders and members in an environment where expertise and ideas are exchanged.

Feedback identifies blind spots which may have been overlooked by leaders, as well as ensuring plans are realistic and achievable with several people considering areas of improvement.

Other Ways to Get Feedback

- *Feedback or Suggestion Boxes:* Allow members to anonymously submit ideas and suggestions.
- *Town Hall Meetings/Church Business Meetings:* Host town hall-style meetings or listening sessions maybe once per month in which members and leadership can discuss issues.
- *Focus Groups:* Organize small focus groups of members to discuss specific topics. For example, if you would like to get feedback on a youth ministry initiative, your focus group would be comprised of young people to offer a comfortable homogeneity group setting.
- *One-on-One Feedback:* One-on-one conversations with church members offer deeper insights into issues, as well as build rapport with members.
- *Online Forums:* Online forums are effective tools to garner valuable feedback. For instance, much information can be gathered from polls, discussion threads, and comment sections.
- *Feedback Forms at Events:* Immediate reactions can be given with feedback forms or cards distributed at a church event. The participants' experiences are valuable

and will more likely be truthful as the feedback is current.

A combination of these methods promotes collaboration, informed decision-making, transparency, and value. It's an effective way to monitor progress, identify issues, and make adjustments to strategic planning, ultimately leading to successful outcomes for the church's outreach initiatives.

Quantitative and Qualitative Methods of Survey

You can use both quantitative and qualitative survey methods to garner your information.

The quantitative method allows the respondent to be anonymous as you are gauging his/her level of engagement and satisfaction. This kind of survey only collects metrics, it doesn't relay feelings and emotions. These questions usually require a rating from the respondent (Please see *Figure 1*).

The qualitative method allows the respondent to also be anonymous, but this kind of survey collects feelings and emotions. Respondents are allowed to write short answers to briefly describe their experiences and circumstances. The qualitative method is also good for testimonials, and you are more likely to garner the truth from your respondents. These questions require detailed answers (Please see *Figure 2*).

Please note, you can choose to combine both quantitative and qualitative methods for a more comprehensive survey.

Whereas Jesus' methods in garnering feedback did not include social media polls, questionnaires, and surveys, he however utilized personal interactions, questions to his disciples and followers, observing reactions and behaviors, and responding to the needs and requests of those he encountered. Direct interactions with individuals and groups, teaching in synagogues, open fields, and homes, and performing miracles create engagement with both the recipients and his followers.

Figure 1: Quantitative Survey Method
Graphic: Canva.com (Olhahladiy), 2024.

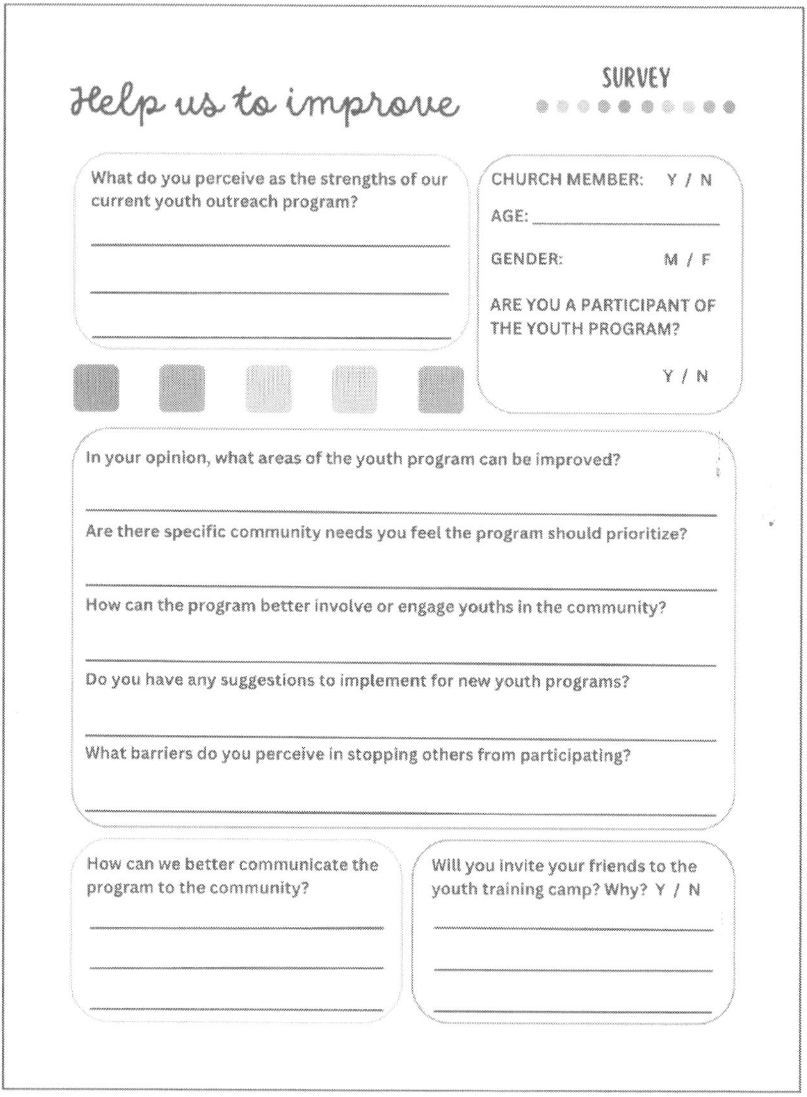

Help us to improve

SURVEY

What do you perceive as the strengths of our current youth outreach program?

CHURCH MEMBER: Y / N

AGE: ____________

GENDER: M / F

ARE YOU A PARTICIPANT OF THE YOUTH PROGRAM?

Y / N

In your opinion, what areas of the youth program can be improved?

Are there specific community needs you feel the program should prioritize?

How can the program better involve or engage youths in the community?

Do you have any suggestions to implement for new youth programs?

What barriers do you perceive in stopping others from participating?

How can we better communicate the program to the community?

Will you invite your friends to the youth training camp? Why? Y / N

Figure 2: Qualitative Survey Method
Graphic: Canva.com (Claudia Gutierriez), 2024.

CHAPTER FOUR

GOALS

A goal is an objective or aim an individual or organization wishes to achieve by a definitive timeframe or within a period of time. There are various types of goals, but they all fall within the following timelines - short-term, medium-term, and long-term.

Tailoring goals within this kind of timeframe helps leaders to develop a comprehensive plan for the church overall.

Short-term goals are usually initiatives that can be launched within 0-12 months, such as increasing attendance by 10% through targeted outreach and invitation campaigns. As a targeted effort, this is a realistic and achievable objective. Therefore, short-term goals should be bite-size in order to achieve them in such a short space of time.

Medium-term goals (1-3 years) are sometimes a continuation of short-term goals. If the initiative was successful in its first year, it's wise to continue or expand from 'launch' to 'maintain' mode. Therefore, picking up where we left off on increasing church attendance by 10%, to expand this initiative, the church can choose to enhance its presence in the community by extending its services through youth ministry. While the church can attain 10% increased growth, incorporating youth-oriented events enables the church to reach a new demographic.

Long-term goals (3+ years) are for the long haul. They expand the church's impact and outreach sustainably. In this case, the church has already established itself in the neighborhood and has successfully increased its attendance through community programs and a thriving youth ministry outreach. To become a stable, sustainable staple in the community, an impactful long-term goal is the establishment of a Christian school or daycare center to provide educational and childcare services rooted in Christian principles.

This kind of goal planning is effective in illustrating a progression of the church's mission and vision.

SMART Goals

Employing the SMART approach in goal-setting and strategic planning is usually recommended for any organization. A church employing this approach to its programs and initiatives is an effective way of being more mindful and decisive when planning. SMART is an acronym for setting objectives that are Specific, Measurable, Achievable, Relevant, and Time-bound.

Specific: Your goals should be clear and focused. Therefore, instead of setting broad goals such as "increase church attendance", try instead to be more specific by applying a numerical value to the increase, such as "increase church attendance by 15%". You can even be more specific by deciding to "increase attendance by 15% among young adults".

Measurable: Using the numeric value (15%), makes this goal measurable. A measurable metric such as numbers, percentages, even dollars, serve as quantifiable indicators that the organization can use to measure success and track progress.

Achievable: Setting realistic and attainable goals prevents feelings of frustration, and they more likely lead to success. Therefore, consider your church's available resources such as funding, staffing or volunteer support, etc., when determining your goals. You should also take constraints or limits into consideration. Nothing more frustrating than setting a goal that cannot be attained because the organization is restrained by laws and regulations.

Relevant: Goals should align with your mission and vision and relate to your strategies and core values. Unifying your priorities reinforces the purpose of your organization. Therefore, if youth ministry is a strategic priority, then it is only relevant to create goals toward increasing youth activity and engagement.

Time-bound: Time-bound also means timely. Goals with deadlines or timelines help organizations to set priorities and become more organized in their operations. For example, "increase attendance by 15% among young adults in the next 6 months", is a goal with a timeline. This dictates the timeframe for the initiative to be launched and carried out. Once the 6 months have ended, the church can decide if it wishes to continue or discontinue the initiative.

SMART GOALS

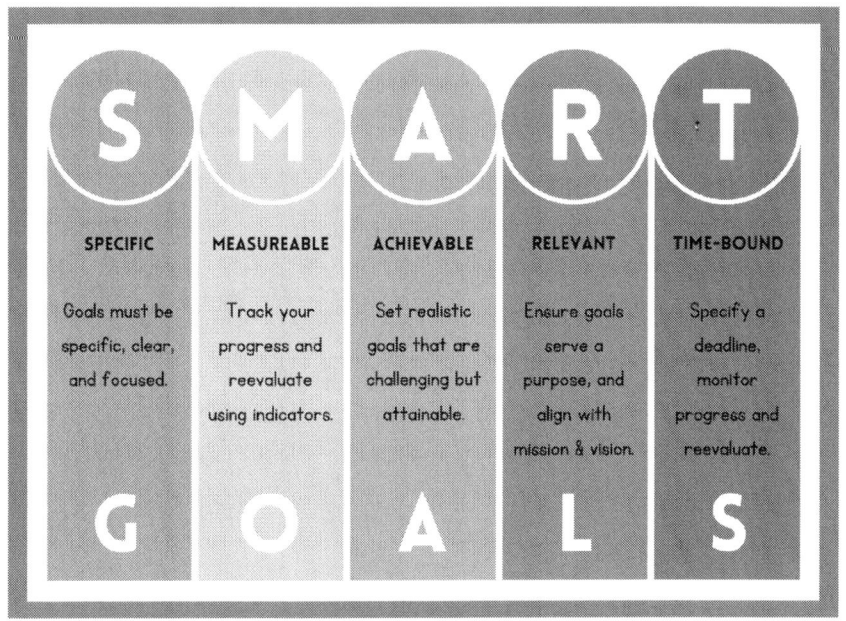

SPECIFIC	MEASUREABLE	ACHIEVABLE	RELEVANT	TIME-BOUND
Goals must be specific, clear, and focused.	Track your progress and reevaluate using indicators.	Set realistic goals that are challenging but attainable.	Ensure goals serve a purpose, and align with mission & vision.	Specify a deadline, monitor progress and reevaluate.

Graphic: Canva.com (Teach Cheat), 2024.

Again, we are seeing that SMART goals are aligned with both the mission and vision of the church. Church leaders can use these well-defined and focused goals to not only lead effectively but also to track progress. Employing the SMART approach assists church leaders in creating a goal-oriented church culture by cultivating focused and mission-driven attitude and behavior in the members.

Finally, using the SMART approach brings clarity and focus, accountability, and alignment to the church's daily operations and indicates where efforts should be directed.

Practical Exercise: *Utilizing SMART Goals in Community Outreach*

Utilizing SMART goals for any program is an effective way to ensure your plans are focused and achievable. SMART goals can be applied to your community outreach program. Let's pretend your church is launching a nutritional cooking program, and you would like community members to attend. Here is how you would apply SMART goal setting:

- *Specific:* Clearly define the objectives of your community outreach program. This includes having a

specific number of community attendees you would like to participate in your program. Maybe your intended number is 20. Your goal would be to "recruit 20 community attendees for the cooking class to be held on Sunday afternoons."
- *Measurable:* How will you know you are meeting this goal of 20 attendees? You will next establish a system to track the numbers. In this case, a simple attendance list for every class is all that is needed. This tracks the number of attendees for each week.
- *Achievable:* Your goal must be achievable. Is it possible to get 20 students from the community to attend your cooking class? To achieve this, take into consideration who the classes are targeted to, and do you have the resources to make it happen?
- *Relevant:* Your efforts must be relevant to the community and should align with your mission and vision. Consider whether your initiative will fulfill a need within the community, for example, if there is food insecurity, hosting nutritional cooking classes may increase the number of participants you receive, especially if students get to eat and receive a bag of groceries after the class.
- *Time-bound:* Your program should have a clear timeframe for it to be sustainable. Decide how long your church may be able to run this cooking program for. You may decide that it is seasonal, or if you are partnering with a local food distribution then maybe you can run the program for longer. Either way, there should be a time frame in mind.

By setting SMART goals for your community outreach program, your efforts are more specific and achievable, and you are more likely to fulfill the needs of your community.

A Practical Business Guide for Church Planning & Community Outreach

EXERCISE: What are the SMART goals for your church or community outreach project?

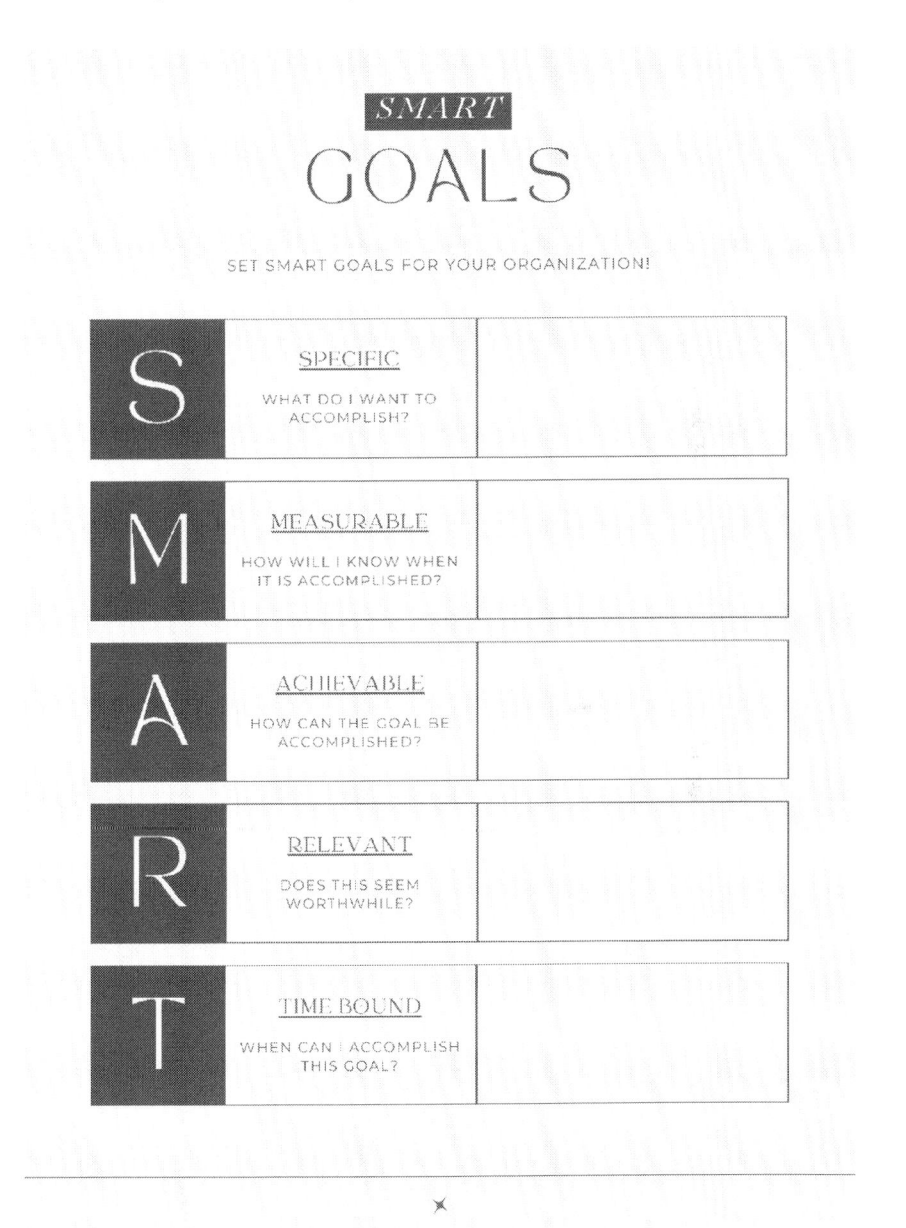

SMART GOALS

SET SMART GOALS FOR YOUR ORGANIZATION!

S — SPECIFIC
WHAT DO I WANT TO ACCOMPLISH?

M — MEASURABLE
HOW WILL I KNOW WHEN IT IS ACCOMPLISHED?

A — ACHIEVABLE
HOW CAN THE GOAL BE ACCOMPLISHED?

R — RELEVANT
DOES THIS SEEM WORTHWHILE?

T — TIME BOUND
WHEN CAN I ACCOMPLISH THIS GOAL?

"Cream Coach Minimal SMART Goals Planner Workbook Worksheet", (2024).

CHAPTER FIVE

CREATING A GOAL-ORIENTED CHURCH CULTURE

Involving stakeholders by motivating and empowering them to achieve the goals of the church means equipping them to make informed decisions. A positive work culture is also reinforced when SMART goals are employed. This gives stakeholders an opportunity to be part of a culture that progresses, achieves, and celebrates small and large wins.

There are several elements involved in creating a goal-oriented church culture. It should be noted that this is a continuous process. It's not a one-time implementation, but instead it's a steady process of improving, reviewing, and refining of these elements toward a sustainable culture. Therefore:

1. The continuous improvement of your church's SMART goals by feedback and evolving of needs, circumstances, and opportunities, provides a collaborative community in which members become involved in the decision-making process. This fosters commitment to goal setting and mission-driven achievements. It should be noted that this greatly impacts stakeholders' understanding of the mission and vision of the church, as well as the church's outreach ministries and programs.
2. The continuous transparency of the church's goals and expectations empower your members by involving them in the planning and implementation process. More interest and commitment are shown when church leaders communicate. Decide on the most effective channels of communication for your church community, such as newsletters, email blasts, bulletins, etc.
3. The utilization of members' ideas and talents fosters an engaged community. Imagine the level of involvement church leaders will see when members are active participants in programs and initiatives that they have recommended or in which their skills are being utilized.

4. Having adequate resources to carry out the mission and vision of the church is paramount. Minimize frustration and disinterest in programs that are ill-equipped with lack of proper support and resources. First, provide training for members to effectively carry out their tasks. Secondly, find proper support and resources that will provide for the needs of your programs, such as reach out to food distribution agencies that can assist in stocking the church's pantry. This creates a sustainable initiative and maintains the commitment of members who wish to donate their time to serving this ministry.
5. Always celebrate the success and progress of reaching milestones and clearing goals. This includes publicly acknowledging stakeholders and teams for their participation. This kind of appreciation and encouragement cultivates teamwork.
6. Getting feedback from individuals opens up an effective channel of communication and collaboration. Therefore, promote cross-functional collaboration between members and leaders, and between teams for diverse perspectives, talents, and skills.
7. Foster a spirit of camaraderie for the whole team. Therefore, church leaders should lead by example in demonstrating commitment in pursuit and participation, and your members will follow suit. As a result, everyone embraces the idea of working together toward growth and impact.

Building church culture takes time. It should be considered as a long-term goal and should not be taken lightly. It's very effective because it models behavior of teams and leaders. As new members become part of your community, church culture plays a significant role in shaping their attitudes toward being a team-player.

CHAPTER SIX

ASSESSING THE CHURCH'S POSITION
(THE SWOT ANALYSIS)

It is always important to know how your church is positioned in the minds of your stakeholders and the community. Is it a haven where members find comfort? Is the community aware of the church's existence, and is it a place where the neighborhood comfortably embraces?

Are you tapping into the strengths of your members and leadership, and improving the weaknesses that may hinder the church's ability to effectively fulfill its mission and vision? How does your church measure up against other churches in the community in relation to community outreach? Are you taking advantage of opportunities within the community and addressing threats that may impact church growth?

To address these concerns, it is important to conduct a SWOT Analysis (strengths, weaknesses, opportunities, threats).

The church's SWOT experience

Here are some common considerations of strengths, weaknesses, opportunities and threats a church may encounter. Of course, factors such as size, location and community demographics should also be considered:

Strengths
- Strong community engagement.
- Effective leadership.
- Vibrant worship services that resonate with members and visitors, which may account for high attendance numbers.
- Diverse ministries catering to various age groups, interests, and needs which may account for the strong community engagement.
- Engaging and vibrant church culture.

- Strong partnership ties with community organizations and local businesses that serve as resources to help the church become more effective in its outreach.
- A dedicated team of volunteers. This helps the church to be able to contribute and make a greater impact within the community.

Weaknesses

- Low and/or declining attendance rate. This indicates challenges in retaining and attracting new members.
- Leadership challenges which may be as a result of a lack of leadership direction and quite possibly poor leadership skills.
- Limited resources, which may include financial constraints and staffing or volunteer shortage. This limits the church's ability to expand its ministries.
- A lack of or ineffective communication with stakeholders. Part of building a collaborative church culture is engaging everyone in transparent and clear communication.
- Lack of diversity may prove to be challenging in increasing attendance numbers. Homogeneity in cultural groups, for example, may hinder the church's ability to be inclusive.

Opportunities

- Access to new members and the expansion of programs via community outreach.
- Chance to gain or work with valuable resources such as food banks, shelters, or counseling services.
- Utilizing technology for virtual worship services such as online social media platforms like YouTube provides a viable mode in which to connect with a wider audience.
- Youth programs such as camps, classes or young people events are great ways to connect to the youth of the community.
- Furthermore, offering GED classes, lifestyle workshops, and bible classes can strengthen engagement.
- Environmental and sustainability workshops and events, such as community clean-up events to engage more people.

Threats

- Decreased attendance due to various changes in demographics (people migrating to other regions), societal trends, and the natural progression of mortality within an aging congregation.
- The financial constraints of members (such as layoffs or challenges in making ends meet) can cause a decline in tithing and donations, resulting in instability in funding programs and ministries.
- Some churches find themselves embroiled in legal issues such as property disputes, regulatory changes, or litigation. This can cause a strain on funds.

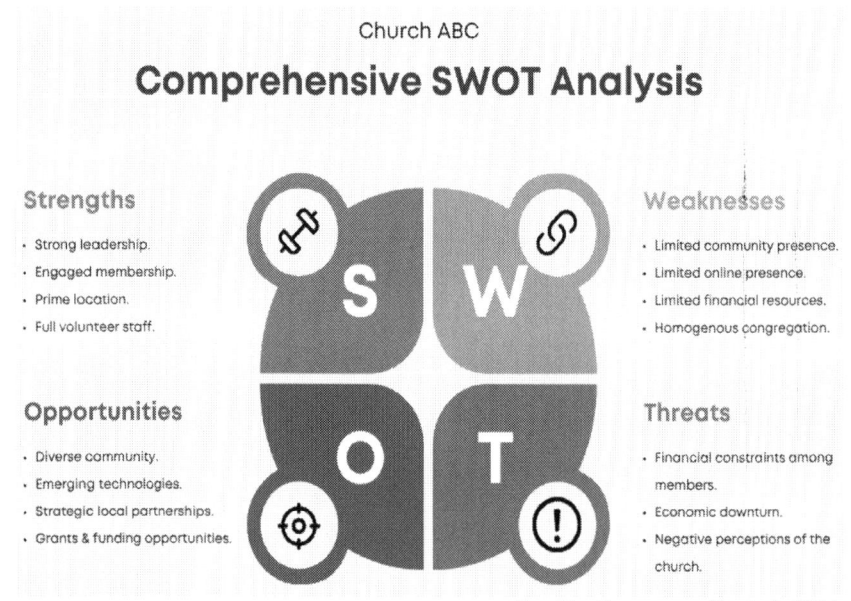

Church ABC
Comprehensive SWOT Analysis

Strengths
- Strong leadership.
- Engaged membership.
- Prime location.
- Full volunteer staff.

Weaknesses
- Limited community presence.
- Limited online presence.
- Limited financial resources.
- Homogenous congregation.

Opportunities
- Diverse community.
- Emerging technologies.
- Strategic local partnerships.
- Grants & funding opportunities.

Threats
- Financial constraints among members.
- Economic downturn.
- Negative perceptions of the church.

Graphic: Canva.com (Antler), 2024.

It should be noted that strengths and weaknesses are internal factors the church can address effectively and strategically, while opportunities and threats are external factors beyond the church's control. Addressing the Weaknesses and Threats and capitalizing on the Opportunities of your SWOT should align with the mission and vision, and even the goals of your church and its initiatives.

Conducting a SWOT Analysis at this stage of the planning process, helps the church to strategically position itself, and to effectively develop its projects and outreach by leveraging and capitalizing on strengths and opportunities, and mitigating and addressing weaknesses and threats.

The Importance of a SWOT

Conducting a SWOT analysis is important for several reasons:

- Conducting a SWOT provides a framework for planning for strategic positioning and making informed decisions by assessing the internal strengths and weaknesses and evaluating the external opportunities and threats.
- A SWOT analysis allows the organization to mitigate risks early on before they develop into major problems. This is known as risk management.
- The directive potential of the SWOT analysis helps the organization to prioritize its goals, which results in allocating resources toward goal-oriented initiatives. This is very impactful as both the mission of the organization and the allocated resources to carry out this mission are effectively aligned.
- Conducting a SWOT promotes collaboration and innovation as stakeholders work together to strengthen the organization's internal infrastructure and monitor its external environment, thereby enhancing their strategic positioning and success.

In Matthew 9:35-38, Jesus and his disciples used this approach by responding to the needs of those around them by leveraging their faith in God and the financial resources of those in the group, by empowering those who were lacking, by taking advantage of the abundant opportunities for ministry, and by acknowledging the need for additional laborers (an obvious awareness of the ministry's limitations or threats to the effectiveness of the overall mission).

The insights gained from the SWOT analysis will enable leaders to make targeted and strategic decisions for both the church and its initiatives.

EXERCISE: Complete a SWOT analysis for your church.

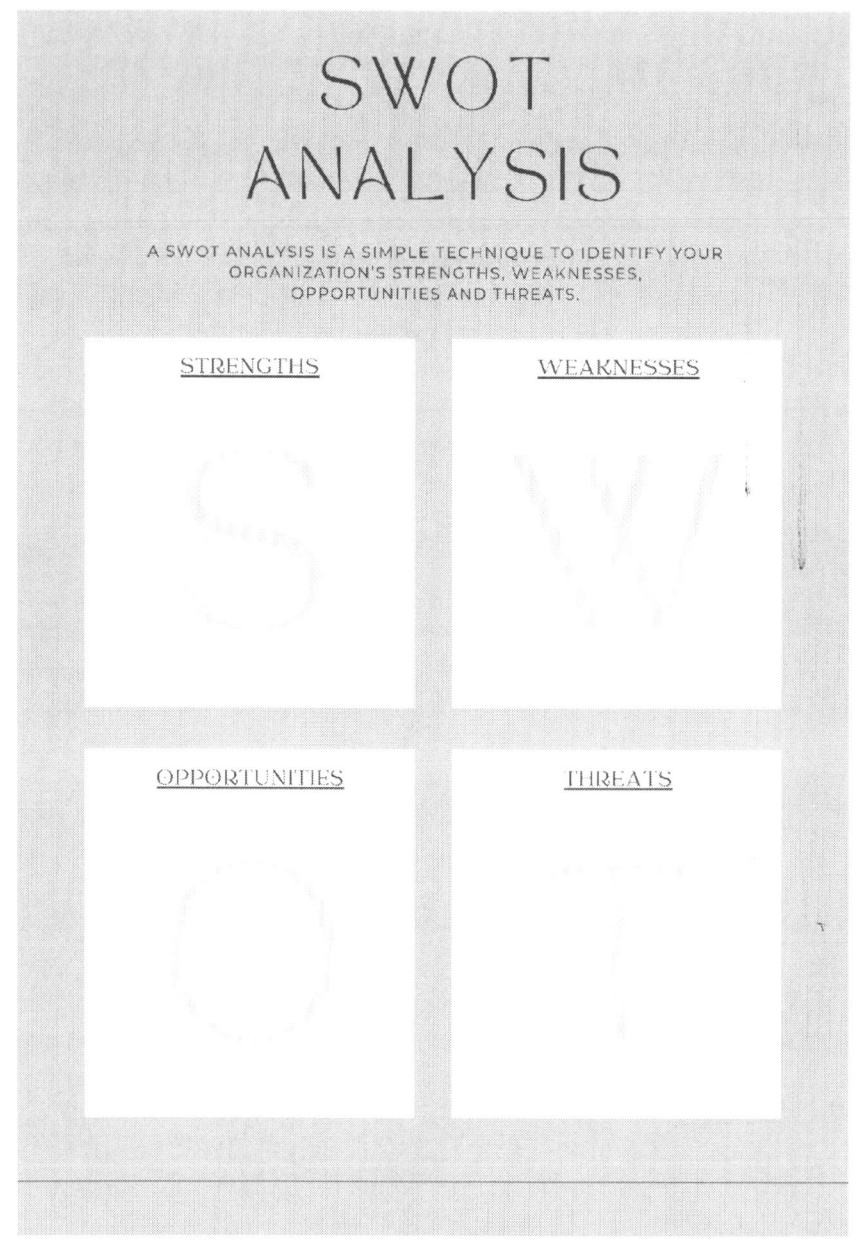

SWOT ANALYSIS

A SWOT ANALYSIS IS A SIMPLE TECHNIQUE TO IDENTIFY YOUR ORGANIZATION'S STRENGTHS, WEAKNESSES, OPPORTUNITIES AND THREATS.

STRENGTHS	WEAKNESSES

OPPORTUNITIES	THREATS

Canva.com (2024). "Cream Coach Minimal SWOT Analysis A4 Document".

CHAPTER SEVEN

THE PLANNING BUDGET

Everyone knows that without the funds to get your projects and plans off the ground, they are as good as dead. Therefore, it is imperative for church leaders to not only plan, but to talk about money.

Budgeting not only helps to enable the church to determine how much money is allocated to various projects, but it also serves as a guideline on expenditure. Budgeting is a part of financial stewardship and provides a framework for financial management and discipline. As a result:

- Church leaders are stewards of the church's resources and members entrust funds donated to be allocated responsibly to create a financially stable environment that supports effective ministry planning and implementation.
- Church leaders are financially accountable and therefore should be transparent in the use of all financial resources.
- Church leaders are strategic planners who responsibly utilize the church's financial resources to meet the mission, vision, and goals of the organization.

Overall, budgeting helps the church to operate within its means, to invest in initiatives that align with its mission and vision, and to provide stability and sustainability in which the church could carry on its work.

It is important to budget for necessary resources such as materials, equipment, facilities, wages for human labor, and even compensation and/or stipends for volunteers. Programs and initiatives need funds to sustain and maintain them over time. Financial resources also enable the church to engage in outreach, such as aiding the needy and serving others. It is also important for the finance team to take sinking funds into consideration when budgeting.

Sinking Funds

Sinking funds are present in every organization's budget. They are a part of the long-term financial planning, and therefore in a church's budget they are reserved funds set aside for specific future expenses or capital projects. As a result, the organization can cover major expenses without dipping into its immediate revenue, fundraising, or donations. Some examples of sinking funds in a church budget may include:

1. *Building and Equipment Maintenance and Repairs:* These are assets which require ongoing maintenance, repairs, and renovations, such as church facilities, roof repairs, HVAC repairs or upgrades, maintenance of the church van, and the audiovisual equipment, etc.
2. *Capital Improvements:* Organizations set aside funds for larger capital projects such as expanding church facilities or constructing a new building in a new space (such as a community center), renovating existing spaces, or purchasing new equipment.
3. *Debt Repayment:* Almost all organizations have some kind of debt repayment, and funds set aside to repay loans or debts incurred by the church for previous capital projects (such as construction loans) is a great way to utilize reserves without interfering with immediate available funds.
4. *Emergency Reserves:* Funds reserved for unforeseen emergencies such as natural disasters, major equipment failures, and/or unexpected financial challenges.

Putting money aside purposely is not only proactive, but it also helps organizations to maintain financial stability, and ensure the long-term sustainability of their ministries and facilities.

Therefore, the finance officers must be knowledgeable in their work of accounting and budgeting to effectively align, allocate and mobilize funds to meet the financial needs of the organization. The followings skills are necessary:

- **Double-Entry Accounting:** Understanding double-entry accounting reflects maintaining a balance of:
$$Assets = Liabilities + Equity.$$

This is also known as the Balance Sheet Equation, which has a list of the organization's *yearly* assets and liabilities. Please see balance sheet template at the end of the chapter (page 48).

- **Maintaining Accounting Charts:** Knowledge of creating and maintaining a systematic list of all the accounts, categorized and used to track all financial activities, such as bar charts and line graphs to paint an overall picture of the organization's health for the quarter or the year.
- **Financial Statements:** Preparation and interpretation of statements such as the yearly balance sheet, and *monthly* income and cash flow statements detailing income and expenditure, and profit and loss (pp.49-50). This is to assess the organization's financial health and performance on a monthly and yearly basis.
- **Accrual Accounting vs. Cash Accounting:** Know the differences between accrual accounting of revenue and expenses when they are incurred, and cash accounting, which only records revenue and expenses when cash is used or exchanged. "Accrual accounting provides a more accurate view of a company's health by including accounts payable and accounts receivable." While cash accounting, which is mainly used by small businesses and sole proprietors, does not accurately record the true financial health of the company (Morah, 2023).
- **Budgeting & Financial Planning:** Financial forecasting and budgeting monitor financial performance and help teams to make informed decisions about resource allocation and spending.
- **Knowledge About Funding Resources:** This includes having knowledge about donor compliances and/or restrictions, as well as bearing the responsibilities for funding accountability.
- **Compliance and Reporting:** Familiarity with regulatory requirements and reporting obligations for nonprofit organizations, including tax filings and adherence to Generally Accepted Accounting Principles (GAAP) or other accounting standards.

- **Grant Management:** Knowledge of accounting principles related to donor contributions, gift restrictions, and grant management, including tracking grant expenditures, reporting requirements, and compliance with grant terms and conditions.
- **Technology Skills:** Finance personnel should know how to use accounting software systems to record transactions, generate financial reports, and streamline accounting processes.

By possessing a strong foundation in these accounting fundamentals, the financial team can effectively manage the organization's finances, maintain an ethical conduct, transparency and accountability, and strategically support the organization's mission and objectives. **PLEASE NOTE:** For a more in-depth understanding of budget and actual income and expenditure statement, follow the case study with worksheets in the workbook (Module 4, p.14).

Factors to consider when establishing the overall church budget.

When establishing the overall church budget, other than thinking about how the programs are aligning with the mission and vision of the church, church leaders should also consider the following key factors:

- *Income sources.* Where will the primary source of the church's finance come from? Would it only rely on tithing and offerings? Or will it incorporate a combination of sources such as fundraising, grant requests, etc.?
- *Expenses.* Nothing kills planning than unexpected and unbudgeted expenses. Consider all the possible operational costs, outreach expenses, debt, maintenance, and miscellaneous costs.
- *Evaluate the Financial Health* of the church before deciding on launching a project. Can the church financially sustain such a project?
- *Member Participation Count.* Is everyone on board? How many volunteers are there, and do you have to hire extra personnel or experts to lead the project?

- Are there enough funds to meet the community's needs?
- Is your budget flexible enough to accommodate changes, emergencies, and unforeseen circumstances?

Factors to consider when establishing the church budget in relation to marketing and community outreach.

An outreach budget will vary according to the project, the size of the congregation and the community, and of course what financial resources are available. Consider the following:

- Salaries, compensation, or stipends for the project's personnel.
- Program expenses which include supplies and materials for the program.
- Transportation costs such as fuel for vehicles or public transportation expenses for your volunteers.
- Rental fees for venues or equipment.
- Printing costs for marketing materials, such as flyers, posters, or brochures.
- External advertising expenses such as posting an ad in the local newspapers, or on the local radio station. You should also factor in the costs for running social media campaigns.
- Costs associated with training volunteers and staff, as well as educational workshops that your personnel may need to attend.
- Miscellaneous expenses for unforeseen emergencies, and unbudgeted additional costs.
- Technology costs such as creating an extra website specifically for the outreach program.

It is important for churches to prioritize their outreach efforts and have accessible funds to launch, implement, and sustain these initiatives. Regular monitoring and evaluation of the budget ensures correct spending and stewardship, transparency and accountability, and sustainability.

ATTENTION: Notice, elements within the church budget vary from the community project budget (see pp. 49-50).

However, after all these considerations, organizations can find themselves in a challenging financial position in meeting the needs

of their initiatives or programs. Here are the most common reasons for this:
1. *Limited Budget:* If the church is operating within a limited budget, this may constrain its ability to fund various outreach programs and initiatives, especially since the church relies primarily on donations from its stakeholders and fundraising efforts to support its ministries.
2. *Fluctuating Revenue:* The church's revenue stream may fluctuate due to factors such as changes in membership count, economic downturn affecting members' financial contribution, or seasonal variations in giving, for example, people tend to give less during summertime when most families are away and in September because of back-to-school costs. This makes budgeting during these seasons unpredictable.
3. *Rising Costs:* Inflation and rising cost of living, cause operating expenses to also increase over time. As a result, the church may struggle to keep its commitment to serving the community. This impacts the long-term sustainability of its outreach programs.
4. *Resource Allocation:* If there are several competing demands for limited resources, then the church must prioritize how it allocates its resources. Some programs will be impacted. This can be a difficult choice.
5. *Funding Gaps:* Despite the church's best efforts, funding gaps or finance shortfalls can happen, and these gaps hinder the sustainability and scalability of the church's outreach efforts.

Here are some budgeting mitigation strategies that can help to alleviate these financial challenges or help to close the funding gaps:
1. *Diversification of Revenue:* The church can explore diversifying its revenue streams, instead of relying solely on membership offerings. It must seek grants from government and private institutions, host fundraising events, and establish partnerships with local businesses or organizations to generate additional income and other resources.

2. *Employ Proactive Financial Planning and Budgeting:* Implementing a robust financial plan includes putting aside funds in reserve and miscellaneous accounts, as well as prioritize spending on more strategic goals that will also help to bring in further income such as hosting auctions and craft fairs that will enable ticket sales and booth rentals.
3. *Stewardship and Transparency:* Including the members in some of the decision-making processes, as well as in the brainstorming process, not only encourages support and engagement, but also demonstrates responsible stewardship and transparency. Members may have great ideas or available resource information on closing the funding gap!
4. *Volunteer Engagement*: Don't underestimate leveraging the time, talents, and resources of volunteers within the congregation and community. This can help to supplement the church's financial resources by reducing costs for labor, activities, and administrative tasks.
5. *Collaboration and Partnerships:* Collaborating with other churches, nonprofit organizations, government agencies, and community stakeholders can pool resources, share expertise, and leverage collective impact to address community needs more effectively. By working together with others, the church can amplify its outreach efforts and achieve greater financial sustainability.

While adequate funding supports the sustainability of the mission, how can churches acquire additional funds other than tithing and offerings to cover all these necessary costs and expenses? Here is a list of funding-raising ideas church leaders can use to help meet their budgeting goals:

- *Special Offerings.* This includes:
  - *Mission Offering* for support of mission trips, outreach projects and evangelism.
  - *Building Fund Offering* for improvement projects, renovations, and expansions of the church facilities.

- *Benevolence Offering* for assisting families who are in need or facing financial hardship, and/or emergency situations.
- *Holiday or Seasonal Offering* for occasions in which the church wants to host a special event such as Thanksgiving or Christmas dinner for the members and the community.
- *Special Project Offering* for any project or initiative that requires financial support beyond the regular budget, or beyond the regular offering.
- *Fundraising Events.* This includes hosting events such as:
  - *Dinners/Banquets* – attendees can purchase the tickets to cover the price per plate, and all profitable proceeds would be donated to a special project.
  - *Concerts and auctions* to engage the wider community.
  - *A Fun Run or a Walk* can be a very engaging event in which participants raise funds through sponsorships or registration fees.
  - *Community Yard Sales* are the best way to bring a community together. Church and community members can donate gently used items, and all proceeds will be donated to a community outreach initiative. If people know they are donating to a worthy cause that they will in turn benefit from, they are more likely to give.
  - *Host a Craft Fair* – encourage local artisans and vendors to sell their handmade or homemade goods, holiday decorations, gifts, and baked goods. While the sellers keep the proceeds from their sales, the church benefits from booth rentals and sales commissions.
- *Online Giving Platforms.* Use apps and the church's website to secure donations.
- *Crowdfunding Campaigns.* Start a GoFundMe crowdfunding campaign to secure donations for a specific project.

- *Brand Merchandise.* Church-branded merchandise such as t-shirts, mugs, and tote bags can be sold on the church's website or as part of your GoFundMe campaign.
- *Bake Sales.*
- *Grants.* Apply for grants and funding from city and government agencies that help non-profit organizations.
- *Community Partnerships.* It's always good to partner or collaborate with local businesses to help the local community.
- *Church Rummage Sales.*
- *Concession Stands* at community events, games, and even state fairs, offer the opportunity to sell branded merchandise, snacks, and baked goods.
- *Online Auctions* offer the opportunity to sell donated items.
- *Sponsorship.* Local businesses can sponsor an event or an initiative. Local businesses look for opportunities to advertise and build awareness. This is a reasonable trade.

There are many more fundraising ideas and opportunities that church leaders can use to raise funds to meet their budgeting goals and support their various ministries.

The Bible teaches that everything belongs to God, and we are stewards of the resources entrusted to us (Psalm 24:1). We are required to be responsible stewards, and this includes the faithful management of our finances. We are advised to plan diligently and not hastily (Proverbs 21:5), underscoring the importance of being wise with our resources.

SAMPLE CHURCH BALANCE SHEET

Church Name: _____ Date: _____

Balance Sheet - Summary of Years 1 to 3
chubalsh.xls

Assets

	Current Assets	Present	EOY - 20__	EOY - 20__	EOY - 20__
101	Checking Acct				
102	Checking Acct				
103	Missions Checking				
111	Savings				
112	Savings				
113	Missions Savings				
114	Designated Funds				
121	Books, Tapes etc. for sale				
131	Pledges not yet received				

	Fixed Assets				
501	Land				
502	Building				
503	Parsonage				
504	Other Houses				
511	Furniture & Equipment				
512	Autos, Vans, Buses				

Liabilities

	Current Liabilities (1 year or less)	Present	EOY - 20__	EOY - 20__	EOY - 20__
801	Church Land & Building				
803	Parsonage				
805	Autos, Vans, Buses				
811	Other Notes/Debt				
812	Other Notes/Debt				
813	Other Notes/Debt				

	Long Term Debt				
861	Church Land & Building				
862	Autos, Vans, Buses				
863	Parsonage				
864	Other Notes/Debt				
865	Other Notes/Debt				
866	Other Notes/Debt				

(c) NFCU 2002

FreeDownloads.net (2015).

A Practical Business Guide for Church Planning & Community Outreach

Sample Monthly Budget

JAN FEB MAR APR MAY JUN
JUL AUG SEP OCT NOV DEC

INCOME	BUDGET	ACTUAL
Tithes		
Special Offerings		
Misc. Offerings		
Fundraising		
Gift Offerings		
TOTAL		

SAVINGS	BUDGET	ACTUAL
Reserves		
Building Fund		
TOTAL		

EXPENSES	BUDGET	ACTUAL
Salaries		
Allowances		
Administrative		
• Phone		
• Insurance		
• Utilities		
• Literature		
• Postage		
• Advertising		
Ministries		
• Youth		
• Music		
• Worship		
Administrative		
TOTAL		

SINKING FUNDS	BUDGET	ACTUAL
Maintenance & Repairs (Building)		
Equip. Replacement		
TOTAL		

DEBT	BUDGET	ACTUAL
Loan Repayment		
Mortgage		
TOTAL		

SUMMARY	BUDGET	ACTUAL
TOTAL INCOME		
TOTAL EXPENSES		
TOTAL SAVINGS		
TOTAL SINKING FUNDS		
TOTAL DEBT		
REMAINING		

Canva.com (2024), Kamala. "Monthly Budget Journal".

Sample Community Outreach Monthly Budget for Food Pantry

(JAN) (FEB) (MAR) (APR) (MAY) (JUN)
(JUL) (AUG) (SEP) (OCT) (NOV) (DEC)

INCOME	BUDGET	ACTUAL
Donations		
Grants		
Fundraising		
In-Kind Donations		
Gift Offerings		
TOTAL		

SAVINGS	BUDGET	ACTUAL
Reserves from Grants		
TOTAL		

EXPENSES	BUDGET	ACTUAL
Insurance		
Advertising		
Operational Costs		
• Volunteer Comp.		
• Utilities		
• Transportation		
• Storage		
• Supplies		
Hosting Expenses		
• Event Costs		
• Nutrition Classes		
• Misc.		
Administrative		
Emergency Food Box		
TOTAL		

SINKING FUNDS	BUDGET	ACTUAL
Maintenance & Repairs (Church Van)		
TOTAL		

DEBT	BUDGET	ACTUAL
TOTAL		

SUMMARY	BUDGET	ACTUAL
TOTAL INCOME		
TOTAL EXPENSES		
TOTAL SAVINGS		
TOTAL SINKING FUNDS		
TOTAL DEBT		
REMAINING		

Canva.com (2024), Kamala. "Monthly Budget Journal".

CHAPTER EIGHT

THE MARKETING OF COMMUNITY OUTREACH

Community outreach is usually a planned approach or initiative which is designed to both engage and meet the needs of a targeted demographic. The main aim of community outreach is to build relationships while meeting the needs of this specific group of people. Sounds a lot like marketing, doesn't it?

While a church is not in the business of selling its services, it can however use the principles of marketing, such as employing promotional strategies, tactics and even marketing channels to enhance the growth of the church and to retain membership engagement. Organizations market their products and/or services by promoting and selling, by selective pricing, and by employing various distribution channels. As with any other aspect of business operation, the marketing aspect must also align with the company's mission and vision. The church is no different. Therefore, the church's community outreach strategy should align with its mission and vision, goals, and objectives.

Community outreach and marketing, while different, can work together to successfully communicate the church's purpose with a strategic approach to its targeted demographic. For example, the purpose of community outreach is to serve the local community. However, the church can employ marketing strategies to promote its campaign, build awareness, and communicate its mission to the community. This is done by advertising, branding, using social media to communicate purposefully.

How does this work?

Typically, church leaders brainstorm a great community initiative. However, most churches become stuck in the idea phase because no one knows how to reach the target audience, and the effective approach to utilize.

First, the initiative is usually targeted to the surrounding community of the church. But how well does the church know the community? Communication flows both ways in marketing. While the church communicates its identity and offerings to encourage participation and involvement, the church needs the community to reciprocate in order to understand and connect with the community. This can be done via community surveys which are distributed in-person for needs assessment. Also feedback mechanisms such as suggestion boxes and comment cards are used regularly to gather visitors and community members' opinions. This is highly effective, especially if the comment cards have a section for the visitor or community member to state his/her needs. Through careful data analysis, churches can gather information on the types of needs that are outstanding within the community. Once gathered, church leaders can then engage in informed decision-making and program planning because they are connected with the community.

Secondly, leaders must then decide on the channel with which to reach the community. Since community outreach is typically a hands-on, service-oriented activity of volunteers engaging with people, leaders must decide on the most effective and successful approach. The approaches vary and they involve utilizing the church's website, social media, newsletters or bulletins, local media, printed materials such as flyers and posters, online advertising, and even local partnerships. Using a combination of these promotional channels can help the church to reach a wider group of people. One really effective approach is the church bulletin or newsletter, as it contains important details such as event dates, updates, locations, and contact information. However, a more promising use of the newsletter is the inclusion of stories and testimonies that are compelling and that will garner the attention of its readers. This speaks volumes for churches looking to make a soulful connection with the community.

Finally, churches should not be afraid of employing marketing tactics to build awareness and create impact. Imagine having a great project in mind and launching it, only for it to receive little to no participation because the church failed in its marketing efforts.

Employing the Principles of Marketing into Community Outreach

Let's take a deeper look into the strategic approach to marketing. This involves implementing the basic framework of the principles of marketing – the 4Ps – product, price, place, promotion, also known as the marketing mix. Management of the marketing mix helps to create value by strategical positioning and influence.

But how can a church employ the marketing mix when there's no tangible product or service on which to place a price tag?

Product refers to a tangible good and/or a service which is launched to meet the needs of a specific group of people. It's usually priced according to costs, competitor's pricing, and other pricing strategies. The distribution channel (place) is selected according to easy accessibility to customers; and it is promoted or advertised persuasively to ultimately increase sales.

Since marketing and community outreach are similar in some respects, such as in their primary purpose to reach a target audience, using strategies and plans to meet needs, build awareness, and create impact to retain engagement, churches therefore, should employ marketing strategies to communicate their value proposition effectively.

Therefore, integrating the main principles of marketing into a church's community outreach planning can enhance the effectiveness of outreach efforts and increase the impact of ministry initiatives. Here's how:

Product

Ministry offerings are various services churches offer to their members and the community. Any initiative or program that identifies and supports the needs of the stakeholders, offers value, and aligns with the church's mission and abilities, can be considered as a product offering. Such offerings may include, but are not limited to, soup kitchens, educational programs, and youth ministries.

Price

Churches strive to offer their programs for little or no cost, and this is to allow for easy accessibility. The focus is on value, benefit, and impact as no price can be placed on spiritual value. Churches cut costs by relying heavily on volunteers who, through teamwork, participate and engage in community projects and activities. The exchange is priceless.

Place

Church leaders must know key locations within the community where their programs can have the greatest impact. This is important because it should also be the place where the target group, they wish to reach is accessible. This may include physical locations such as community centers and schools, and/or digital platforms such as social media, and the church's website. Finally, partnerships with local organizations help to establish community ties and networks.

Promotion

Of course, no marketing strategy or community outreach is successful without promotion. Promotion or advertising your initiative can take many forms, from printed materials to online banners and posts. Whatever the marketing channel used, the key to successful promotion is crafting the right message that is compelling to your audience, utilizing the most effective channel for that audience, and following-up through engagement and communication.

There is much to be achieved by integrating the principles of marketing into community outreach planning. Not only does it communicate the church's value to the community, but it also opens up the opportunity for community engagement and long-lasting relationships, as well as the church positioning itself within the community.

CHAPTER NINE

MARKETING CHANNELS FOR THE CHURCH

Now that you know the fundamental principles of marketing your community outreach programs and initiatives, you now must consider how the church can establish and engage its digital and physical presence to its targeted demographics. Marketing drives the success of any business. Churches are no exception.

First, leverage a mix of marketing channels to promote the church's initiatives. You're not restricted to one channel or one marketing tactic. Interacting online includes organic marketing efforts, paid advertising campaigns, blogging, vlogging, and social media banners and posters.

Second, bear in mind you will be fostering long-lasting relationships, especially through organic marketing outreach, therefore choose the channels that most likely represent the preferences of your target audience. For example, Linkedin is an unlikely social media channel as it is more business oriented; however, if you are looking for businesses which partner with or sponsor non-profits, then consider using Linkedin to connect with professionals.

Your social media manager should create engaging content that will capture the audience's attention. In the long run, being able to engage and communicate with your audience through relatable posts is key to growing a large following. This is known as organic marketing. For example, posting inspirational messages often can be a helpful resource for many online users to come back to time and time again, and it provides the opportunity to interact in comment threads. Don't forget to use hashtags and geotags to broaden your church's exposure to the world. Always keep your audience informed to retain their engagement.

Here are a variety of ways to do this:
1. *Social media:*

a. Facebook - Create a page to post about church and community events, run ads, and host live events (using Facebook Reels).
   b. Instagram - Share photos, stories, and IGTV videos, and engage with hashtags.
   c. Twitter - Post updates, share news, and engage in conversations with your followers.
   d. YouTube - Post sermons, testimonials, and other church-related videos.
   e. LinkedIn - Share church activities and connect with professionals.
   f. Pinterest - This platform allows you to create boards for inspirational quotes, events, and community outreach.
2. *Email Marketing:*
   a. Email Newsletters - Build an email list to regularly send updates, news, and inspirational messages.
   b. Event Invitations - Send out invites to church events and programs.
   c. Automated Email Campaigns - Use MailChimp to create automated email campaigns. This is great for follow-ups with new visitors, and for donor engagement.
3. *Church Website:* Your church website does not have to remain static, having the same information all the time. Use this space to frequently update your audience about upcoming events. Add enriching testimonials of members of the church on the church's website or its blog, that can also be shared on social media. Blogging includes articles, stories, sermons, and insights on various topics. Optimize the church's website, using SEO, to attract visitors beyond the social media platform.
4. Share details about volunteer projects and events. Most people search online for volunteer opportunities. Also work with local colleges and universities to host internships and community service projects for students.

5. *Virtual events:* Host virtual events, for example health webinars, mental health coaching, or educational workshops such as how to write a college entrance essay. Post these on social media to promote the event for greater participation.
6. Other online hosting events include **informative videos** with relatable matters that cover common needs or issues, such as homelessness and food insecurity; **hotline and support services** for families in crisis; **interviews** with health and employment experts; and **virtual parenting webinars** and family financial education. Valuable educational content not only puts your church on the radar as a resourceful tool people can use, but leveraging the online platform to carry out this mission will also extend the church's outreach for increased membership.
7. Work closely with community partners and local businesses and highlight their support. A church involved in the community is a church that becomes the community's beacon of light. Highlighting the work of the church and its partners on social media via photos and videos, provides a glimpse of the church's outreach efforts to the community and those beyond it, therefore increasing the chances of partnering on a larger scale for more outreach initiatives.
8. *Streaming platforms:*
    a. Live Streaming Services - Broadcast services and events live on platforms like YouTube Live, Facebook Live, and Vimeo.
    b. Webinars - Host online workshops, Bible studies, and Q&A sessions to answer burning questions about religion, family, faith, etc.
    c. Podcasting - Share sermons, discussions, and interviews on platforms like Spotify, Apple Podcasts, and Google Podcasts.

Online sermons, devotions and a prayer ministry will offer your church the opportunity to move spiritual services outside the local community and enrich a wider group of people. Imagine tech resources such as going

Live on YouTube as an extended arm of the church. Live stream community events with live interviews or participants enable your online followers to participate virtually.
9. *Online advertising:*
    a. Google Ads - Run search and display ads to reach a broader audience.
    b. Facebook Ads - Target specific demographics and interests with paid ads.
    c. Instagram Ads - Use sponsored posts and stories to promote events and messages.
10. *Create an online community:*
    a. Online Forums - Create discussion boards on platforms like Reddit or church-specific forums.
    b. Slack or Discord - Set up channels for different groups within the church.
    c. WhatsApp or Telegram Groups - Consider using these platforms for quick updates and community building.
    It would be wise to share these platforms with the locals within your community.
11. Fundraising platforms like GoFundMe or Kickstarter allow the church to communicate its goals and projects.
12. *Church app:* Imagine creating your own app with features like event calendars, sermon archives, and donation tools.
13. *Educational platforms:* Consider offering online courses on platforms like Udemy, Teachable and Google Classroom. The courses can be about any topic, and they can be free of cost or for a fee. Free courses, however, are useful to garner more engagement.

Utilizing **offline marketing** channels are just as important and effective as online channels. For example, print material is very useful in engaging the local community and keeping residents abreast of upcoming events. These include banners, A-signs, posters, and flyers. Of course, they should be colorful, vibrant, and creative.
1. *Traditional Media:*

a. Newspaper Ads - Place advertisements in local newspapers to promote events and services.
b. Radio Spots - Use local radio stations to advertise church activities and to air weekly sermons or Bible studies.
c. TV Advertising - Create and air ads for your events on local television channels.
d. Billboards - Rent billboard space to announce major events such as a crusade. More people within the community are likely to see this.
e. Local Bulletin Ads - Advertise in community bulletins or publications.

2. *Print materials:* Imagine creating and printing your own newsletters and bulletins to be distributed via person-to-person handouts. They are informative and impactful in connecting the church with its community frequently. Use visually compelling photos. Note: Take printing costs into consideration, especially for full color versions. However, to cut costs on your newsletters, distribute them via email marketing. Flyers, posters, and brochures are also more practical for distributing locally such as in libraries, businesses, cafes, and community boards.

3. *Direct Mail:* Up to 10 years ago, direct mail was one of the most effective ways for churches to advertise. However, over time, direct mail has become costly, mainly because of high printing costs of the cards and expensive labor costs for the agency in charge of mailing your cards to the specific zip code. While some churches and non-profits still use this method to 'get more eyeballs' on their advertising, in the long run, it is much cheaper to pursue other offline channels.

4. *Public Relations:* This is a vital department in any organization. Developing and managing a public relations department within your church helps to enhance the relationship between the church and the community. It nurtures engagement and retention through strategic communication; leverages promotional channels to reach the population effectively; and communicates the mission and value of the church to the community. The public relations department can utilize local newspapers and bulletins for

press releases, as well as local radio and TV stations to advertise and for media interviews.
5. *Promotional items:* Create t-shirts to distribute branded apparel to promote the church. Also, give away promotional items such as pens, magnets, and mugs printed with the church's logo.
6. *Signage:* Church signage such as banners and A-signs can be used to announce upcoming events and services. Banners are usually placed in high-traffic areas and A-signs can be placed on the exterior of the church building to draw the attention of passers-by.

Marketing the church's community outreach programs and initiatives are essential to the growth of any church ministry and should be carefully planned with adequate resources (funds and labor) allocated to its success.

EXERCISE: Describe your existing project. What additional marketing strategies would you employ, and why?

CHAPTER TEN

SCOREBOARD (PERFORMANCE OVERVIEW)

Keeping track of the plan's progress is known as score boarding. This includes assessing key performance indicators (KPIs) and progress toward goals. It should be noted that KPIs are measurable values used to evaluate success in meeting benchmarks and preset goals. Examples of KPIs include financial growth, increased production output, improvement in customer satisfaction score (CSAT), employee satisfaction and increased sales conversion rate.

In regard to score boarding church outcomes, KPIs would include measuring success in community outreach and church health such as tracking average weekly attendance, engagement and participation rate in church programs, trends in tithing and financial stewardship, community impact, and member retention. As a result, an organization's KPI will align with its missions, visions, and strategies.

Score boarding is accountable and transparent, and therefore is usually reflected in visual representations such as charts and graphs to communicate goal-reaching updates to leaders and stakeholders, and to provide periodic updates on performance and outcomes.

Typical kinds of score boarding involves dashboard indicators (metrics and data in a visual dashboard format) which are commonly used in businesses; balanced score boarding which measures the success of strategy executions; and performance score boards which show performance metrics. Other score boards include educational, sales and financial to track academic achievements, meeting revenue quotas and profitability, respectively.

Depending on the type of project and community program, churches can employ the following kinds of score boarding to track engagement and impact.

Quantitative KPIs
1. **Project Scoreboards:** Most churches and non-profit organizations use project scoreboards to track and

communicate project progress, milestones, and key deliverables. The visual displays show the metrics for project timelines, task status, budget vs. actuals, and benchmarks. As a result, stakeholders are informed and updated on the progress of the project.

2. **Evangelism Scoreboard:** Every year, churches keep count of new baptisms from evangelistic meetings and outreach campaigns. This scoreboard is usually a goal thermometer poster showing baptismal count. Churches can also keep an attendance of visitors to the evangelistic meeting. This provides insight on evangelistic outreach impact through community engagement. Numbers to the online live streaming should also be noted, and subscriptions should be encouraged.

3. **Members' Growth and Engagement Dashboard:** This kind of scoreboard keeps a tally and measures church growth and engagement by keeping attendance and guest books, and the number of members participating in events and programs. It also observes the participation of new members and visitors.

4. **Financial Scoreboard:** No matter the community outreach project, the financial scoreboard is necessary to keep church leaders on budget. The financial scoreboard is the most popular kind of performance metric used by churches to track performance of fundraising activities, meeting a proposed budget, and achieving the church building fund through offerings. This tool helps church leaders to monitor the church or a department's financial progress. Most church leaders like to use this metric for transparency and accountability. Types of financial scoreboards include:
   - *Budget vs. Actuals Scoreboard* which compares the church's actual financial performance to its proposed budget. It details the church's finance health by comparing income, expenses, and savings. It also tracks or monitors whether the church is sticking to its budget.
   - *Fundraising Progress Scoreboard* is usually used to measure fundraising progress for projects and initiatives such as the church building fund, or community programs. Fundraising events usually have a specific

target to be met, and the scoreboard tracks how much is raised within the specific time period set.
- *Tithe and Offering Tracking Metric* keeps track of tithes and offering over a period of time. Churches usually see an increase in tithes and offering on special occasions and events. The tracker provides insight into the church's financial performance for a specific day.
- *Debt Reduction Scoreboard* is a transparent progression of the reduction of outstanding debt. It shows the amount paid to date and the remaining balance.
- *Savings or Reserve Fund Scoreboard* is a tally of money put aside for emergency or as reserve for unexpected expenses, a 'rainy-day fund'. The scoreboard keeps track of the balance and church leaders can encourage giving by setting a monetary goal amount.

5. **Youth Ministry Scoreboard:** The dashboard allows church leaders to track youth ministry effectiveness and identify areas for improvement. This ministry usually targets the youth of the community in a discipleship program. It includes programs that engage the youth in educational classes, mentorship, Bible studies, and sport and entertainment activities. A community youth project is measured by engagement, and church leaders analyze the data (the percentage of participation and retention) to determine the success of the program or if there is need for improvement.

6. **Digital Engagement Dashboard:** Checking the analytics on the church's website and across digital platforms (such as likes, shares, views, and comments) helps church leaders or the public relations department to assess the impact and health of the church's online ministry.

These quantitative Key Performance Indicators (KPIs) are metrics often used to assess whether the church is meeting its goals and understands the community's needs and problems. But the appropriate metric or scoreboard must be used to track such factors as the number of individuals reached, their engagement and retention in the programs. For example, a pilot food assistance program is an effective way to assess and determine the community's food insecurity. The participation data will indicate whether there is a need for support in addressing food insecurity within the community. Analyzing KPI data and trends, helps to refine the church's outreach strategies, such as where resources should be allocated, what kind of support is needed, how often, whether to seek outside help, and what kind of local and regional networks would be ideal partnerships.

Qualitative KPIs

Qualitative Key Performance Indicator (KPIs) are not measured by metrics such as numbers, percentages, or monetary values. Instead, qualitative KPIs are measured by satisfaction, engagement, and perception.

- **Community Satisfaction:** Church leaders can gain insight into the quality of their outreach program by assessing community satisfaction. This can be done through surveys, feedback forms, focus groups, and personal interviews.
- **Participation Engagement:** A qualitative scoreboard for participation engagement is to measure the level of involvement. This can be done by observations and/or focus group discussions.
- **Testimonial Narratives:** This form of qualitative scoreboard is the most compelling. Narratives and testimonials are about experiences, and nothing speaks volume on success than the testimonies of community members who found your event enriching. It serves as a benchmark because it is a firsthand account.
    o Testimonials are considered authentic because they are personal. They offer genuine perspectives.
    o Testimonials offer an emotional perspective which is very impactful, thus giving them credibility.
    o Testimonials are relatable because they are from one human to another. Therefore, it is easier for people to build trust on the positive experiences of others.
    o Testimonials can empower, motivate, and inspire.

Qualitative scoreboard has the human element to it, and therefore communicates perspectives that are relatable to others. Church leaders can use this emotional element as a powerful tool in their public relations outreach. Therefore, getting written testimonials for the church's website and newsletter or on video for social media outreach, can be impactful in raising awareness and involvement in the church's initiatives.

It is no wonder that there are so many Christians in the world today. The testimonies of the disciples and the people who followed Jesus in the first century of the church, have successfully garnered a huge following over many centuries. Firsthand accounts will always remain the most effective KPI because they are authentic, real-life perspective that leave deep and lasting impressions on its recipients.

Churches are accountable to their stakeholders who like to know that their efforts are successful. Church leaders can use qualitative KPI as support to the quantitative metrics. This is important because numbers cannot provide a look into the emotional nuances like qualitative KPI can. Therefore, both quantitative and qualitative KPIs are necessary for assessing and keeping track of the church's outreach efforts. Furthermore, KPIs inspire church members toward participating in community work and help leadership to make better decisions and refine strategies.

EXERCISE: What KPIs would you utilize? Why?

CHAPTER 11

PRACTICAL COMMUNITY OUTREACH EXERCISES

To garner community members' commitment and engagement, outreach programs must be carefully planned to ensure effective implementation of your organization's initiatives. The objective of your initiative is to harness all possible resources to develop and implement successful programs that address the needs of underserved populations.

As mentioned in the previous chapters, to create more practical outreach initiatives, the organization must:
1. Understand the Community's Needs.
2. Design the Appropriate Outreach Program.
3. Build Partnerships and Collaboration Outside the Sphere of the Organization.
4. Allocate and Mobilize Resources Effectively.
5. Implement and Evaluate.
6. Plan the Next Steps Toward Sustainability.

Understand the Community's Needs

Understanding community needs is very crucial to effective community outreach, and it involves assessing the target audience by gathering information to identify and determine their challenges and priorities.

Assessment: To assess community needs and gather data and information, the use of surveys, interviews, focus groups, and observations are effective in understanding the demographics, their socioeconomic status, health issues, levels of education, housing and employment conditions, and other factors that may be relevant.

Determine Challenges and Priorities: For a particular demographic, needs may vary and are usually prioritized according to the significance of their challenges. An organization can determine pressing needs from the data gathered and once data is collected, it is analyzed for vulnerability.

Know Your Target Populations: Part of understanding the target audience or community is employing cultural competence to respect diversity. This involves showing sensitivity and respect to varying perspectives, beliefs, norms, and values.

Utilize Asset Mapping: It is imperative to recognize the strengths and opportunities existing within the community, such as within local businesses, schools, and regional government agencies to leverage resources.

Design the Appropriate Outreach Program

Organizations are expected to develop well-structured plans to address the identified needs of a specific community or target population. The key steps involved are:

Define Goals and Objectives: All initiatives, programs, and projects begin with a specific mission and vision, and defined goals and objectives. It's the thought of clearly defined specific outcomes the program or project intends to achieve.

Determine Target Population: Identify the specific population or community group which will benefit from the outreach program after taking the time to understand the community and its needs.

Determine Strategies: Based on the identified needs and goals, the strategies the organization utilize will reflect and align with the community. select appropriate intervention strategies to address those needs. For example, a church's pantry intending to meet the needs of a community's food-insecurity would strategize to enroll in local food business partnerships such as supermarkets, grocery stores, and restaurants to receive donations of surplus or unsold food items; as well as establish collaborative partnerships with funding and grant sources.

Develop Program Activities: Planning is one thing, but implementing your plans into actionable steps brings the program to life. These actionable steps include providing services, materials, and deliverables. SMART goals should be applied to program activities.

Evaluate, Assess, and Monitor: Apply KPIs to evaluate, assess, and monitor the effectiveness of the project, using quantitative or qualitative measures, or both.

Determine Sustainability and Scalability: Is the project sustainable and can be scaled over time? Explore opportunities via a SWOT analysis for long-term viability and impact to achieve meaningful outcomes.

Build Partnerships and Collaboration Outside the Sphere of the Organization

Building partnerships and collaborating with other organizations, agencies, and stakeholders maximizes the organization's impact and resources.

Identify Potential Partners: Begin by identifying potential partners whose mission, values, and goals align with those of your organization; and whose expertise such as skilled labor, networks, and resources such as facilities, can be leveraged. This is done by building trust and developing working relationships.

With clearly defined roles and responsibilities for each partnership and effective communication, written agreements and understandings can be established. This kind of collaboration encourages creativity in problem-solving, the development of new and innovative strategies, and the capability of achieving collective goals. It's a win-win situation.

Resource Allocation and Mobilization

This refers to strategic management of available resources and assets.

Resource Allocation: This refers to the process of distributing resources among different programs, projects, or activities which is the main premise of resource allocation. Every day, leaders participate in decision-making on how to best utilize limited resources to gain maximized efficiency. Resources such as financial and skilled labor are usually paramount in developing budgets and plans. Resource allocation is dependent on prioritizing critical needs and maintaining flexibility to changing circumstances and unforeseen challenges or opportunities. There should be transparency and accountability in the resource allocation process.

Resource Mobilization: This refers to acquiring and generating resources such as donations and grants from various internal and external sources to support a specific purpose – in this case, the project's goals, and activities. For nonprofits, mobilization includes engaging human resources in the form of paid or volunteer labor.

Implementation and Evaluation

Part of the program management cycle is the implementation and evaluation of the planned activities.

Implementation: Implementation refers to the process of executing the planned activities, plus following the design and timeline of the plan. It also involves engaging the necessary resources, financial and human, to effectively carry out program activities and tasks, while actively monitoring best practices through quality assurance management.

Evaluation: The systematic assessment of the project's effectiveness includes evaluating the planning, analyzing the data collection, and interpreting evaluation findings against the project's goals. By evaluating the experience, organizations can learn a lot from the results.

Next Steps Toward Sustainability

Ensuring the long-term viability of a project helps to maintain and enhance positive outcomes over time. There are several elements to sustainability such as financial sustainability which involves improving the diversification of funds to prevent reliance on one funding source; building reserves to buffer against disruption in funding; and capability to cultivate new funding sources. Secondly, organizational sustainability ensures the company has building capacity, and is achieved through transparency, accountability, leadership stability, and proper risk management enforcement. Third, project sustainability entails flexibility to make changes and the capability to adopt and innovate, effective stakeholder engagement, and robust monitoring and evaluation. Finally, environmental sustainability not only includes operating sustainably, but also adopting and cultivating innovative practices toward the long term.

Imagine the leadership team of the church gathering together to brainstorm about the next community outreach event. There will be a lot of communication among the members of the group, and much emphasis will be placed on factors such as the mission, vision, and goals of the event, which will impact budgeting and marketing strategies. Of course, the success of the outreach will be determined by the above-mentioned factors, that is understanding your community's needs, building partnerships, etc., as well as, having preset KPIs to gauge your progress. Your team's outreach framework will first highlight the goals of each factor, and the planning team will take it further by filling in the details.

The following are five examples of community engagement focus project frameworks that include these factors:

Program: Mission-Aligned Food Pantry Expansion
- *Mission:* The church will expand its food pantry to meet food insecurity needs in the community.
- *Vision:* To create a welcoming and accessible space where community members can access nutritious food and resources in times of need.
- *Goal-making:* A short-term goal to increase the variety and quantity of food distributed by 25% in the neighborhood within the next year, and over the next 3 years (long-term goal), reach a broader segment of the community.
- *Budgeting:*
  - Enroll the church's pantry in local food business partnerships such as supermarkets, grocery stores, and restaurants to receive donations of surplus or unsold food items.
  - Allocate funds for regional food banks, food rescue organizations, and hunger relief agencies who provide bulk quantities of food at discounted rates.
  - Prioritize utilizing the food banks which are free.
  - Allocate funds for storage (shelving and refrigeration), and signage for advertising.
- *Marketing Tactics:* Promote and advertise the pantry by local flyer distribution and social media. If the pantry is new, consider hosting a grand opening event to raise awareness and attract members of the neighborhood.
- *Success Indicators:* Determine the success of the new pantry outreach by logging the number of community members served and engaged. Another way to measure success is to get feedback from the community via a survey.

Program: Youth Mentorship
- *Mission:* The church will develop a teenage youth outreach and mentorship program that empowers faith and leadership for teen members of the church and the community as future leaders of the church.

- *Vision:* To cultivate an inclusive youth mentorship ministry that nurtures fellowship and spiritual growth of teens who will empower those around them through leadership and service.
- *Goal-making:* Establish a medium-term goal to increase youth engagement in church and by community outreach activities by 40% over the next two years, fostering a sense of belonging and ownership among young people. Create a leadership course in which teens will participate.
- *Budgeting:* Allocate funds for hiring a youth minister or director and organizing youth events and service projects. Host ongoing fundraising events for purchasing curriculum materials for 12-month leadership course and for supporting the first batch of graduate youth leaders via a small monthly stipend.
- *Marketing Tactics:* Conduct a community survey to assess interest and youth needs to determine emotional and spiritual support. Promote the youth mentorship program via social media platforms, school partnerships, and word-of-mouth referrals from current youth members of the church, as well as printed flyers for distribution within the community. Host open house events and youth-led worship services to showcase the program to the broader community.
- *Success Indicators:* Measure success by tracking attendance at youth events and leadership classes. Analyze quantitative data for retention of youth participants. Garner qualitative feedback via questionnaire from parents and youth leaders, and testimonials of spiritual growth and transformation from participants.

Program: Community Garden
- *Mission:* Create a community garden that promotes healthy living and neighborhood inclusivity, and meet the need of community food insecurity
- *Vision:* Establish a community garden which provides fresh produce, nutrition education via cooking classes and nutrition newsletter, and a community eatery and gathering space for people of all ages and backgrounds.

- *Goal-making:* Establish a medium-term goal to cultivate and harvest 500 pounds of fresh produce annually, donating a portion to the neighborhood and utilizing the rest for Sunday afternoon cooking classes which is served in the eatery to the community participants of the class.
- *Budgeting:* Set aside funds to begin purchasing the garden infrastructure such as raised vegetable beds and an irrigation system, soil fertilizer and vitamins, seeds, gardening tools, items for cooking classes such as pots, and promotional materials to advertise the community garden program.
- *Marketing Tactics:* Utilize signage, social media posts, printed materials and person-to-person neighborhood outreach efforts to promote the program. Host a community launch for the opening of the garden, and host harvest festivals to showcase the harvest. Also, photograph and/or video record cooking classes to post online to attract new participants.
- *Success Indicators:* Analyze the log for volunteer hours contributed and the number of participants in the cooking classes overtime. Measure success by tracking garden yield, the amount of food distributed per household, and the community participation rates to determine the impact of donated produce on food security in the community.

Program: Senior Citizen Wellness and Outreach
- *Mission:* Develop a wellness program for seniors which includes nutritional, physical, and spiritual wellness to meet the needs of elders in the community and foster stronger community connections.
- *Vision:* The vision of this program is to create a supportive and inclusive environment for senior citizens of the community, as well as foster a socialization effort for stronger bonds.
- *Goal-making:* Increase senior participation within the church by hosting senior wellness activities to aim for a 30% increase within a year to create enrichment by health classes, exercise, senior socialization events such as bingo games, and spiritual enrichment.

- *Budgeting:* Host fundraising events such as bake sales for hiring a wellness instructor. Seniors can contribute to the fund-raising event by baking pies for the bake sale. Also raise funds for providing transportation assistance.
- *Marketing Tactics:* Most seniors are typically not online. Therefore, promotion should be via printed materials such as flyers, brochures, and newsletters; and word-of-mouth such as targeted outreach to local retirement communities, senior centers, and healthcare providers.
- *Success Indicators:* Measure success by tracking program attendance to social events, exercise programs, and health and spiritual enrichment classes. Also, get testimonials from the participants (that can be later printed in the newsletters to further promote the program to other seniors).

Program: Neighborhood Beautification and Revitalization Project

- *Mission:* Demonstrate God's love and church servitude via a restoration project. Work with members of the neighborhood to beautify and revitalize their physical environment.
- *Vision:* Foster connectivity and inclusivity among neighbors and the church to create engagement via an aesthetic appeal project.
- *Goal-making:* Establish short- and medium-term goals to complete a series of neighborhood beautification projects. Begin first with a clean-up campaign (such as park cleanups). Second, mural installations to add color and visual appeal. Third, create a neighborhood flower garden and socialization space utilizing the abandoned community space in the town square (make sure to receive city permission for the space).
- *Budgeting:* Mobilizing volunteers and resources from the church and surrounding community (determine those interested in volunteering via a survey). Seek partnership with local businesses and/or request funds from the city or other state or regional governmental agencies who provide grants for this kind of project. Budget funds for project

supplies, volunteer coordination, permits, and community engagement activities.
- *Marketing Tactics:* Utilize local media services such as radio and local paper to promote the beautification projects. Social media posts, church newsletters and local advertising at town hall meetings can also get the word out to solicit volunteers and engagement.
- *Success Indicators:* Tracking the project's success can be done by analyzing volunteer participation rates for the clean-up campaign; survey analysis for the mural installations; and qualitative questionnaire for the neighborhood flower garden project. These will determine engagement, resident satisfaction, and sense of community pride.

The programs can be used as a framework for churches to develop community engagement projects that align with their mission, vision, and goals. Budgeting priorities are based on the type of initiative and marketing tactics. The success indicators used will assess whether the initiative addressed the needs of the community, and whether the approach or strategy is successful and impactful.

Other Initiatives

Here is an extensive list of community outreach projects churches can consider implementing within the short, medium, or long-term:

1. *Clothing Closet:* Distribute donated clothing, shoes, and accessories to individuals and families in need of clothing assistance.
   - Consider a professional attire closet to provide professional clothing and accessories for jobseekers and for those advancing their careers.
   - Consider a maternity clothing closet for expectant mothers.
   - Also consider a plus-size closet.
2. *Homeless Shelter:*
   If your church has the space to house the homeless and you can partner with local organizations to provide shelter, meals, and support services for individuals experiencing

homelessness, then here is a list of the types of shelters you can consider implementing:
- *Emergency Shelter:* Provides immediate and short-term housing and basic necessities such as showers, meals, a bed, and a safe environment during times of crisis or extreme weather conditions.
- *Transitional Shelter:* This is a longer-term housing and support service as people work towards permanent housing and stability. Consider also providing training for employment and clothing for interviews.
- *Family Shelter:* Your space may be small but may be big enough to house at least one family who is transitioning to a more permanent home.
- *Winter Shelter:* You can consider operating seasonally such as only during the colder months to provide temporary housing and to protect individuals from the risk of hypothermia and cold-related illnesses.

3. *Job Training and Placement Assistance*
   - Offer job training programs such as skills development workshops.
   - Provide recommendation letters for students who have done voluntary community service at the church.
   - Resume writing, interview preparation, and job placement assistance.
   - Partner with community colleges to sponsor students for vocational training programs in high-demand industries such as healthcare, construction, hospitality, or information technology.
   - Collaborate with free programs and local businesses to support internship and apprenticeship opportunities to students.
   - Organize a job fair and network with local and regional businesses plus staffing agencies to provide a platform for jobseekers to have easy access to job

opportunities. This helps to meet the unemployment needs of the community.
4. *Health and Wellness Programs:* Provide free or low-cost medical, dental, and mental health services to uninsured or underinsured individuals in the community.
    - *Healthcare Resources Assistance:* Support the community, especially the elderly, by helping members to navigate the healthcare system; provide information on access to affordable healthcare services; assist in the enrollment of health insurance programs; and connect with healthcare providers.
    - *Support Groups and Counseling Services:* Facilitate support groups and counseling services to offer a safe confidential space for individuals dealing with health challenges, chronic conditions, mental health issues, addiction recovery, and grief.
    - *Fitness and Exercise Programs:* Fitness programs such as exercise classes, yoga, tai chi, and aerobics provide opportunities for health improvement and community socialization.
    - *Health Screenings and Wellness Fairs:* Collaborate with the community hospital and clinics to host health screenings and a wellness fair, in which the community can participate for free or at a low-cost. Organize dental cleanings, and screenings for blood pressure, cholesterol, glucose, and BMI.
    - *Offer Free CPR Classes:* Host life-saving training classes to members and the community. Acquire a licensed City CPR Instructor to teach these classes.
5. *After-School Programs:* Lots of parents need after-school activities for their children. Offer tutoring, homework help, scientific activities, and mentorship opportunities for children and youth in the community.
6. *Senior Services:* Provide companionship for lonely seniors, transportation assistance, meal delivery, and other support services for seniors living alone or in assisted living facilities.

7. *Parenting Classes:* Offer parenting classes, workshops, and support groups to help parents develop positive parenting skills and strengthen family relationships.
8. *Financial Literacy Workshops:* Provide workshops, seminars, and one-on-one counseling sessions to help individuals and families improve financial literacy, budgeting skills, and money management.
9. *English as a Second Language (ESL) Classes:* Offer ESL classes and language learning support for immigrants and refugees in the community.
10. *Disaster Relief Services:*
    - Provide emergency assistance for families needing short-term help such as shelter and food assistance.
    - Have a support service in place for individuals and families affected by natural disasters, such as hurricanes, floods, and even fires.
11. *Prison Ministry:*
    - Mentorship and emotional and spiritual counseling.
    - Offer reentry assistance for individuals being released and transitioning back into the community.
12. *Addiction Recovery Support Groups*: Facilitate support groups, counseling, and recovery programs for individuals struggling with addiction and substance abuse.
13. *Foster Care and Adoption Support:* Help foster families with resources and advocacy, as well as adoptive parents, and children in the foster care system.
14. *Holiday Assistance Programs:* Coordinate holiday assistance programs to provide gifts, meals, and support for families in need during Thanksgiving, Christmas, and other holidays.
15. *Mobile Outreach Services:* Bring essential services, such as food, clothing, hygiene supplies, and medical care, directly to underserved neighborhoods and populations through mobile outreach programs such as a dental van. This means partnering with a local dentist office.
16. *Environmental Stewardship Initiatives*
    - Environmental Education and Conservation in the form of educational programs, workshops, and

outdoor activities to raise awareness about environmental issues.
- Clean-up projects and recycling programs.
- Energy efficiency upgrade and eco-friendly initiatives.
- Environmental sustainability and stewardship.

17. *Mental Health Support Groups*
    - Counseling services
    - Educational workshops on mental health challenges.
18. *Literacy Programs*
    - Literacy tutoring and reading clubs.
    - Reading book distribution programs such as a reading mobile service.
19. *Community Meals:* Host community meals or potluck dinners where residents can come together to share food and socialize.
20. *Home Repair and Maintenance:* Organize home repair and maintenance projects to assist elderly, disabled, or low-income homeowners with church member volunteers who are skilled in renovation and construction.

EXERCISE: Decide on a new project for your church. Next, create a project framework, using your mission, vision, goals, budgeting, marketing tactics, and scoreboard as your outline.

CHAPTER 12

CONCLUSION

The church's mission, vision, goals, budgeting priorities, marketing tactics, and success indicators play vital roles in fostering community engagement, reaching new audiences, retaining current membership, and creating opportunities for spiritual growth and connection.

The mission of any organization serves as the purpose for its existence. The vision communicates the desired outcome. By setting goals and objectives, the mission and the vision are carried out. In the realm of engaging with the community, reaching new audiences, retaining current membership, and creating opportunities for spiritual growth and connection, church leaders must intentionally budget and invest in areas that align with its mission, and market effectively leveraging several channels. Only after these strategic factors have been put in place, can church leaders know the truth about their outreach efforts by using KPIs (success indicators) as measurable benchmarks for evaluating and tracking their progress.

Churches have a unique opportunity to be impactful, and what better way to do it than to be a guiding light and an instrument of change to those in the surrounding neighborhoods. Jesus fulfilled the immediate needs of the people he met. He is the classic example of the kingdom of God in action. Church leaders must stay true to the mission of the church; that is, they must utilize every available community outreach opportunity to enrich and transform lives and fulfill the ultimate mission of Christ to "go and make disciples" (Matthew 28: 19a, NIV).

NOTES

References

Bible Gateway. New International Version (NIV), 2024. https://biblegateway.com

Cover Design. YaniDwi, (2024). Blue and Yellow Geometric Business Ebook Cover. Canva. https://canva.com

FreeDownloads.net (2015). Church Balance Sheet Template. Website. https://freedownloads.net/balance-sheets/church-balance-sheet-template/

Graphics. Canva.com, 2024. https://canva.com
    Antler, (2024). Orange Modern Business SWOT Analysis Graph. Canva. https://canva.com

    Claudia Gutierriez, (2024). Colorful Pastel Printable Back-to-School Parent Survey. Canva. https://canva.com

    Cream Coach Minimal SWOT Analysis A4 Document. 2024. Canva. https://canva.com

    Kamala, (2024). Monthly Budget Journal. Canva. https://canva.com

    Olhahladiy, (2024). Blue Simple Minimalist Customer Survey Form. Canva. https://canva.com

    Puput Studio, (2024). Red and Yellow Simple Mission and Vision Poster. Canva. https://canva.com

    Teach Cheat, (2024). SMART Goals SEL Poster Colorful Boxes. Canva. https://canva.com

Morah, C. (Updated November 28, 2023). Accrual Accounting vs. Cash Basis Accounting: What's the Difference? Investopedia. https://www.investopedia.com/ask/answers/09/accrual-accounting.asp

OTHER PUBLICATION

Branding Hacks for Successful Digital Marketing A beginner's step-by-step guide with AI Tutorial and an Extensive List of Online Tools & Resources, is written especially for the young entrepreneur. This guidebook is ideal for precollege (Grades 11&12) and college students, as well as for Start-ups. It's comprised of 12 chapters, detailed step-by-step guide, links and online resources, tools, and platforms which students can use to start their brand. Softcover paperback in full color.

Students doing this course will learn:
- To develop and build a brand.
- Understand the concept of bringing a product or service to the target market.
- Establish the brand on social media platforms via digital marketing by effectively harnessing the innovative creativity of artificial intelligence.

Written and designed by Dawnette Blackwood-Rhoomes as part of an online brand marketing course for Udemy and Teachable Learning platforms and can also serve as a stand-alone detailed guide for students and small business owners.
- Course: https://bit.ly/45TIy5D
- Textbook Only: https://amzn.to/3PfsOTZ

Made in the USA
Columbia, SC
14 January 2025